DECODABLE BOOKS

Take-Home Version

Grade 1 ◆ Volume 1

Orlando Boston Dallas Chicago San Diego

Visit *The Learning Site!*
www.harcourtschool.com

Printed in the United States of America

Part number 9997-38085-1
ISBN 0-15-326714-3

2 3 4 5 6 7 8 9 10 085 10 09 08 07 06 05 04 03 02

Contents

DECODABLE BOOK 1
Pat

Fold

Pat

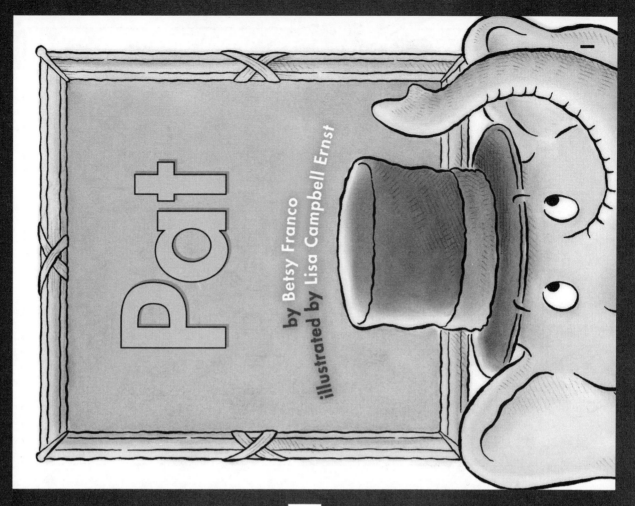

by Betsy Franco
illustrated by Lisa Campbell Ernst

I am Pat.

Fold

Fold

Pat sat. Go, Pat!

Pat sat. Go, Pat!

Fold

Pat

Word Count: 26

High-Frequency Words

do
go
what

Decodable Words*

am
can
Cat
I
Pat
sat
tap

*Words with /a/*a* appear in **boldface** type.

Tap, tap, tap!

Fold

Pat sat. Go, Cat!

What can Pat do?

Pat can tap!

DECODABLE BOOK 1
Nan Cat!

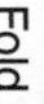

Nan Cat!

by J.C. Cunningham
illustrated by Michael Grejniec

Come here, Nan!

Fold

Fold

Nan Cat sat.

Come here, Nan!

Fold

Nan Cat!

Word Count: 25

High-Frequency Words

come
here
look
up

Decodable Words*

am
at
Cat
I
Nan
sad
sat

*Words with /a/*a* appear in **boldface** type.

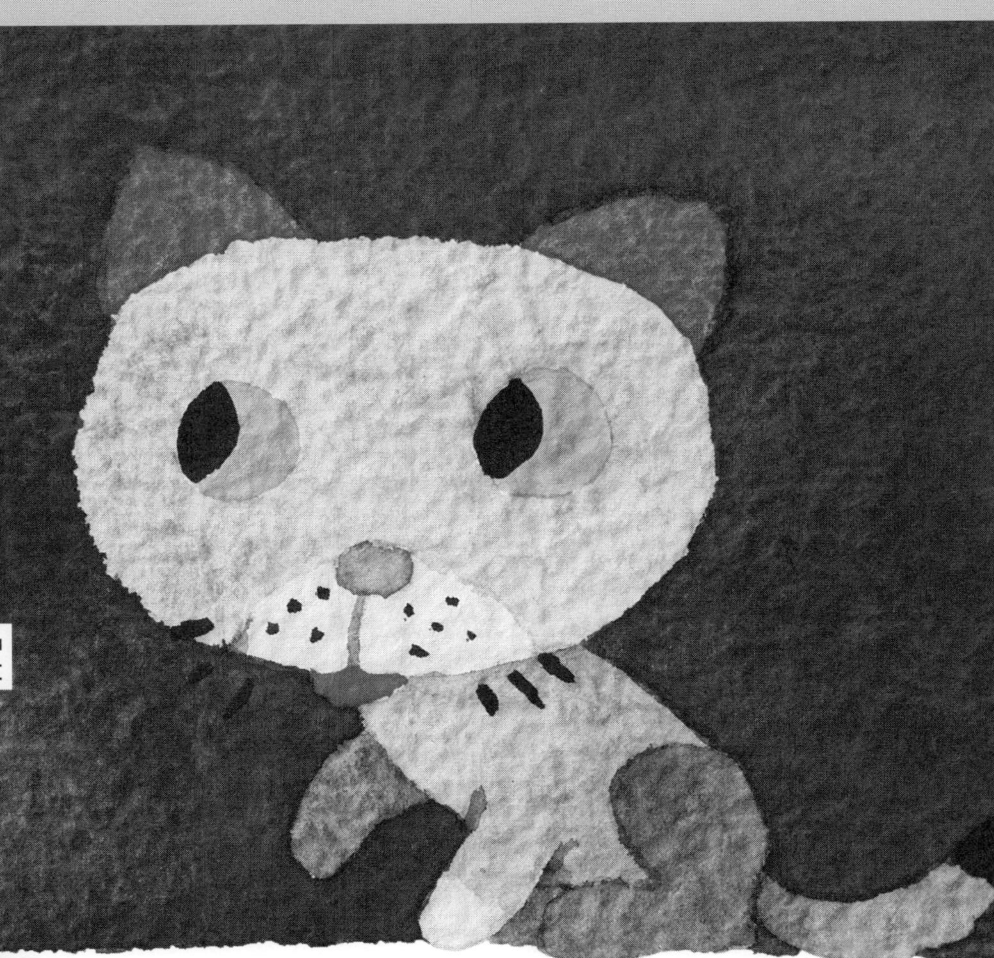

Look at Nan Cat!

Fold

Nan Cat sat up.

I am sad, Nan.

Fold

Nan! Nan!

DECODABLE BOOK 2
Ham? Hat?

Fold

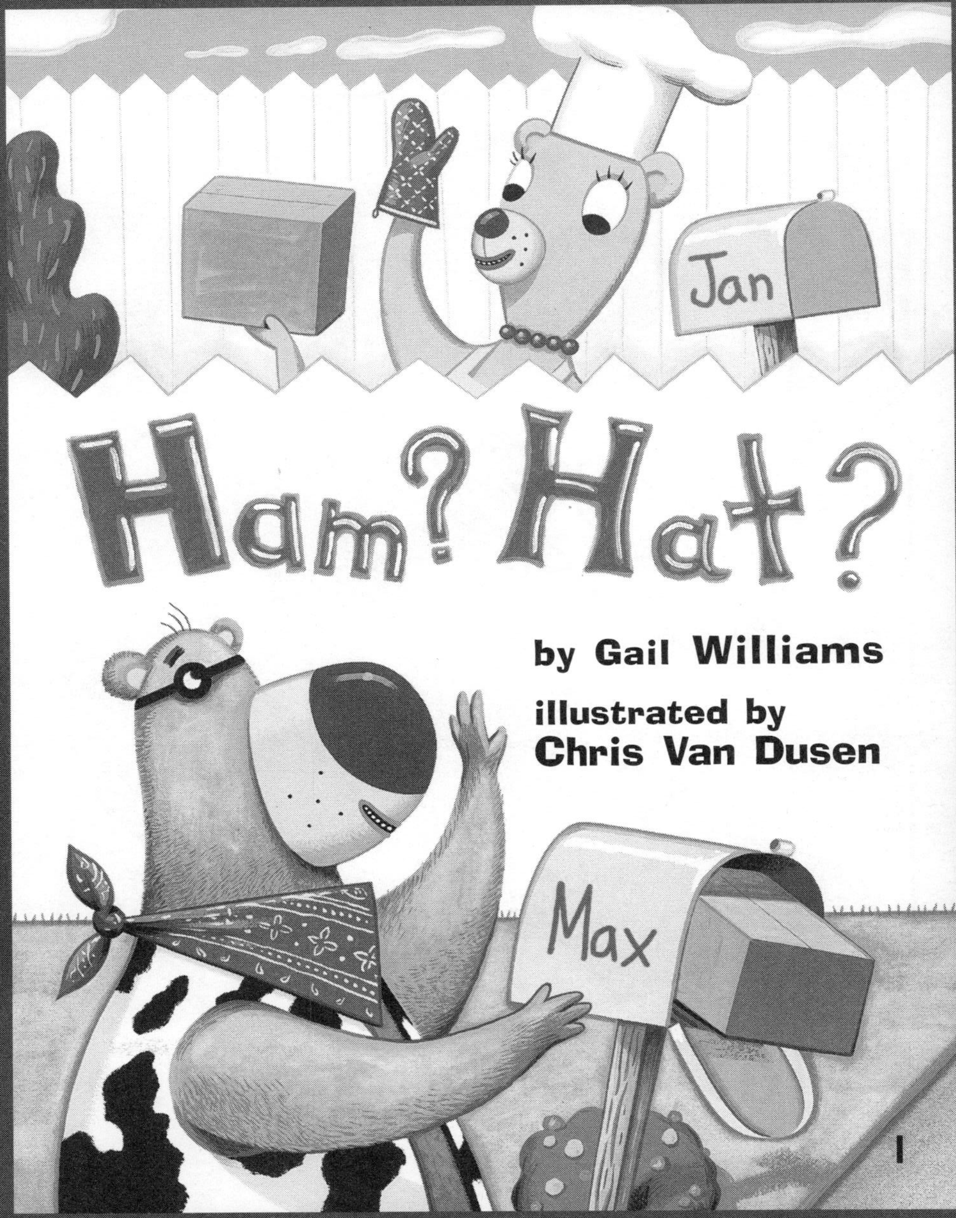

Ham? Hat?

by Gail Williams

illustrated by
Chris Van Dusen

Jan

Max

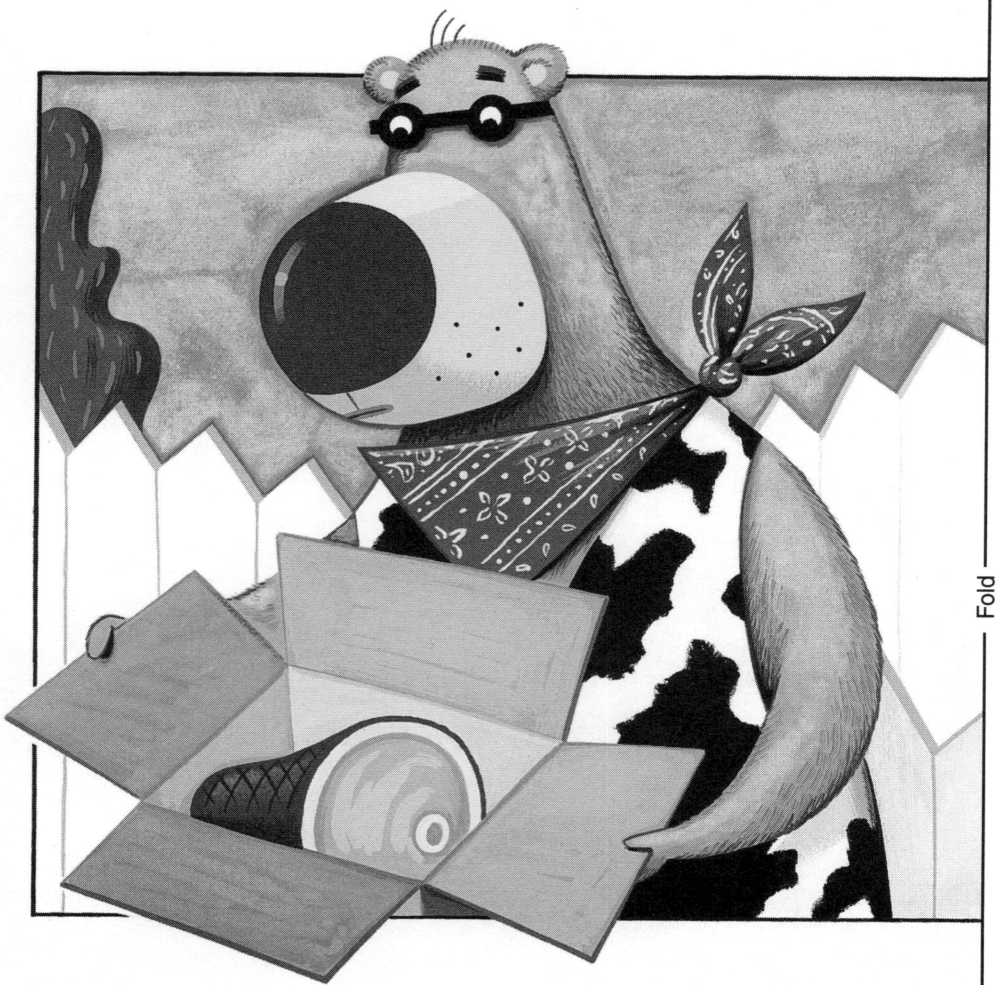

Max had a ham.

Fold

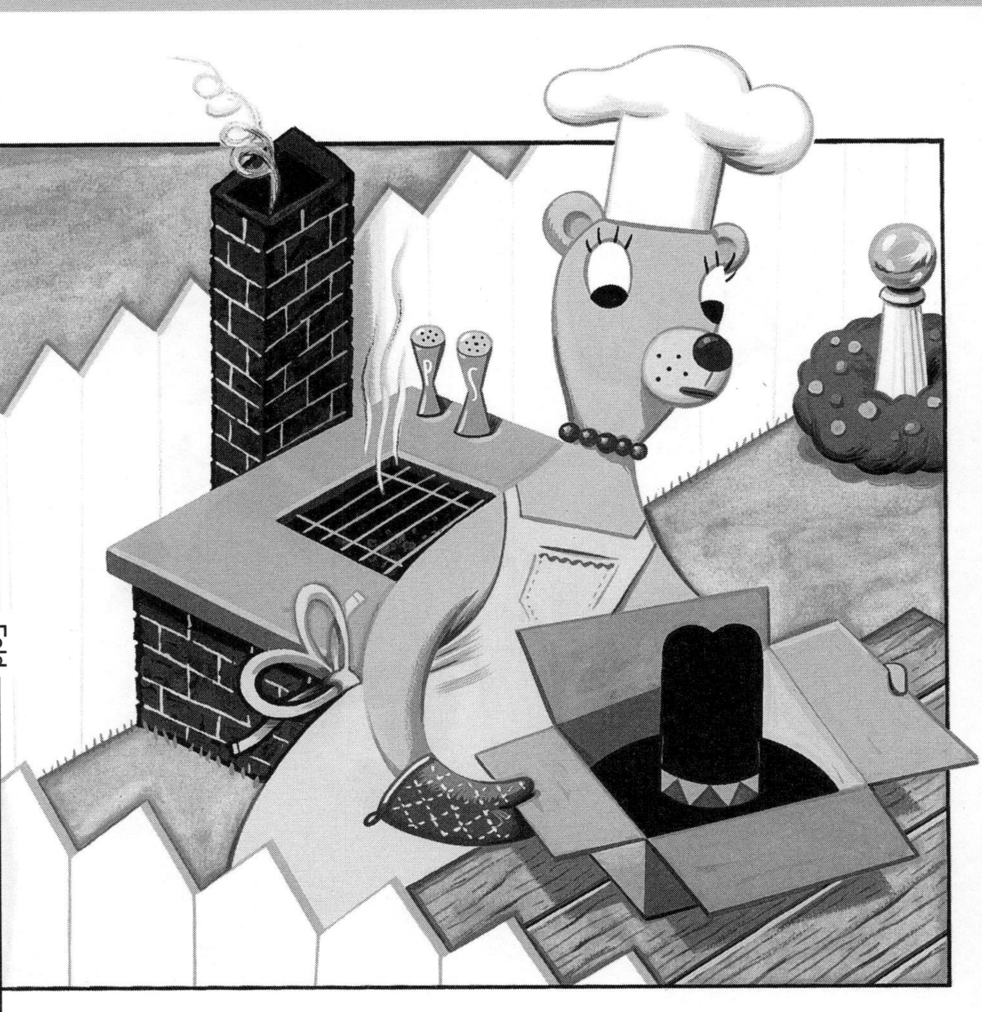

Jan had a hat.

Fold

A ham?

Fold

Ham? Hat?

Word Count: 30

High-Frequency Words

have
the

Decodable Words*

a
had
ham
has
hat
Jan
Max

*Words with /a/*a* appear in **boldface** type.

Max has the hat!
Jan has the ham!

Fold

A hat?

Have a ham, Jan.

Have a hat, Max.

DECODABLE BOOK 2
Tap a Hat

Fold

Tap a Hat

by Mary Hogan
illustrated by Pam Paparone

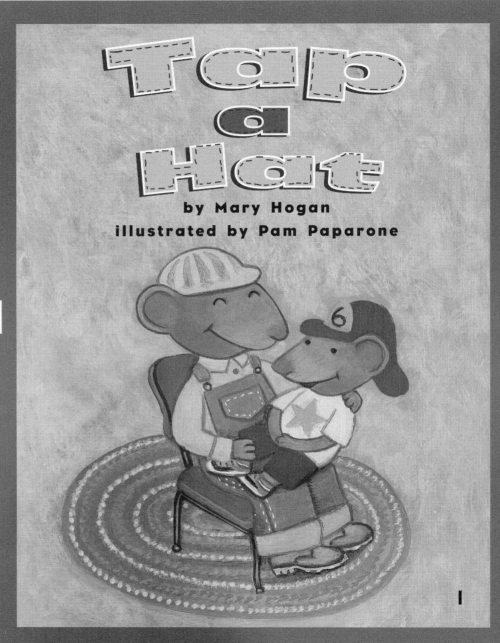

Dad has a hat.

Fold

Fold

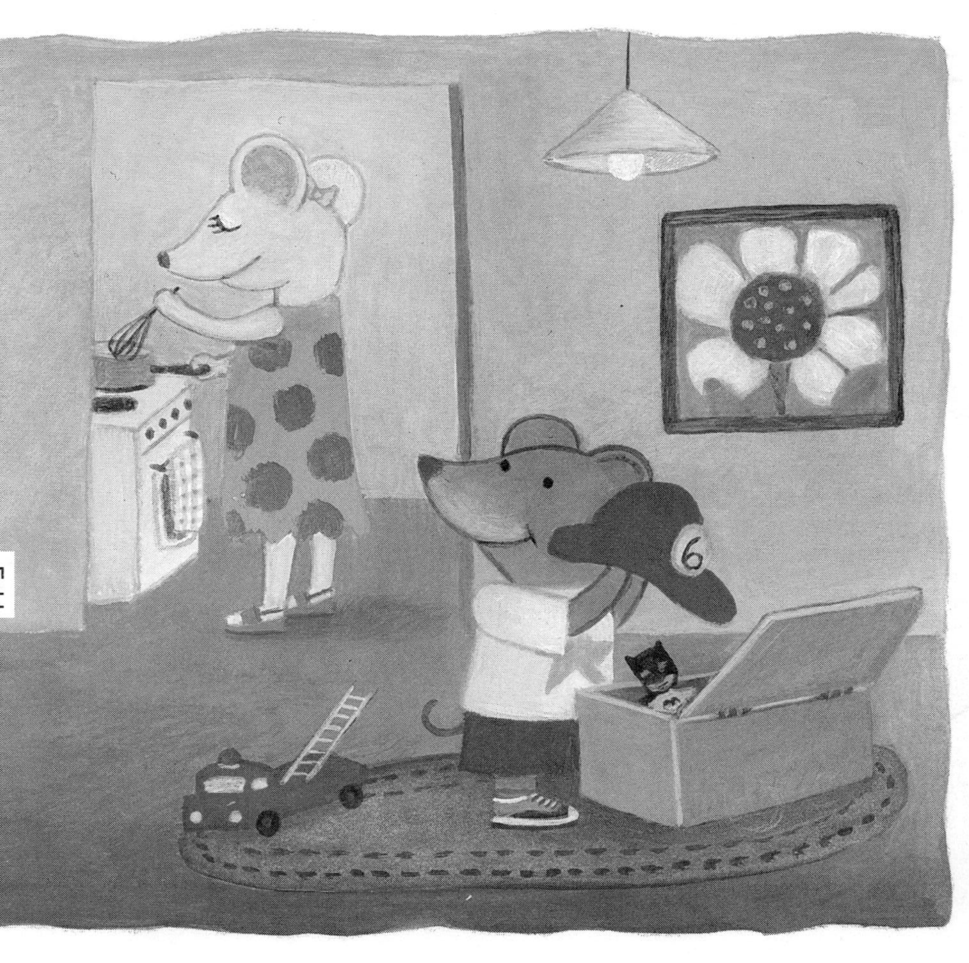

Tad has a hat.

Dad can pat the hat.

Fold

Tap a Hat

Word Count: 32

High-Frequency Words

the
you

Decodable Words*

a
can
dad
has
hat
pat
Tad
tap

*Words with /a/*a* appear in **boldface** type.

Can you tap a hat?

Fold

Pat, pat, pat.

Tad can tap the hat.

Fold

Tap, tap, tap.

DECODABLE BOOK 3
Sid

Sid

by Susan Blackaby illustrated by Nathan Jarvis

Look at what Sid did.
Liz is mad at Sid.

Fold

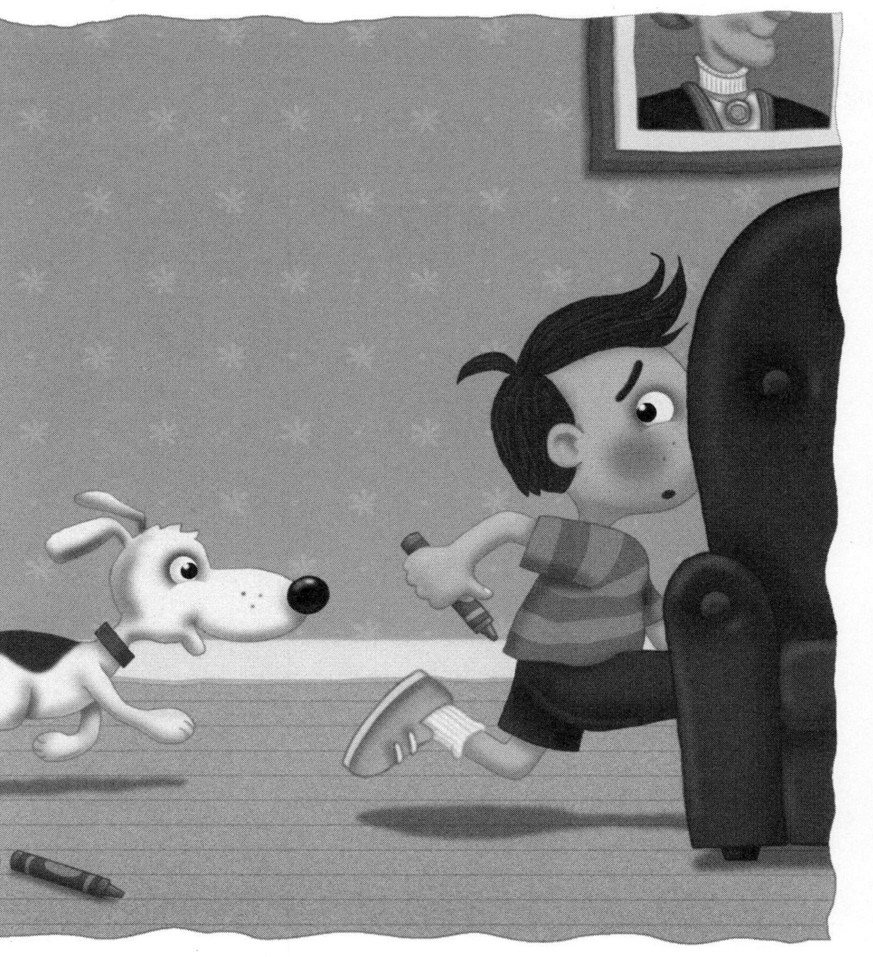

Sid ran and hid. Zip!

Fold

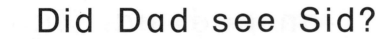

Did Dad see Sid?

Fold

Sid

Word Count: 40

High-Frequency Words

for
here
look
see
what

Decodable Words*

a
and
at
Dad
did
gift
has
hid
him
is
it
Liz
mad
ran
Sid
Tim
Tip
zip

*Words with /i/*i* appear in **boldface** type.

It is Sid!

Sid has a gift for Liz.

Fold

Did Tim see him?

Did Tip see him?

Fold

Is Sid here?

DECODABLE BOOK 3
Tim and Pip

Fold

Tim and Pip

by Lisa deMauro
illustrated by Ande Cook

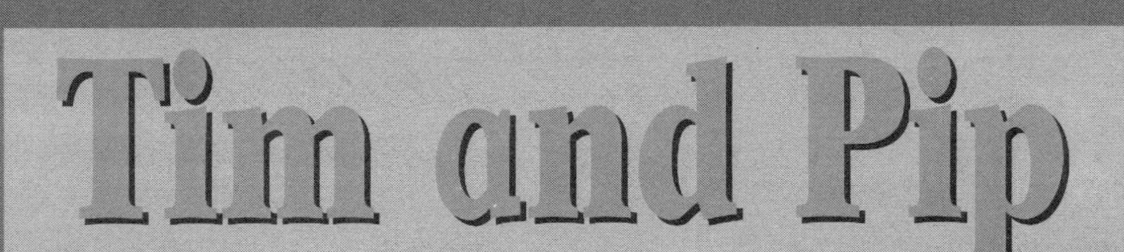

Tim and Pip are pals.

Fold

Fold

Tim sits on a mat.
Tim will have a nap.

Will Pip nap?

Fold

Tim and Pip

Word Count: 38

High-Frequency Words

are
have
on

Decodable Words

a
and
big
has
hat
his
in
mat
nap
naps
pals
Pip
sits
Tim
will

*Words with /i/*i* appear in **boldface** type.

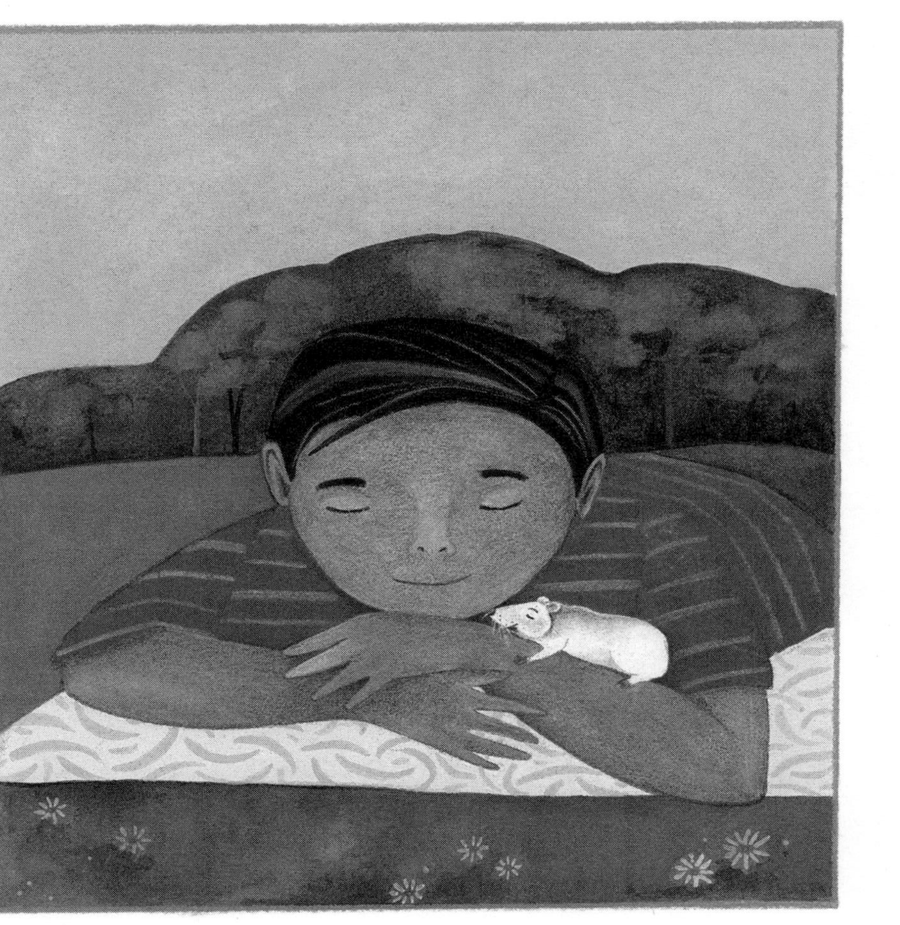

Pip naps on Tim!

Fold

Pip sits in a big hat.

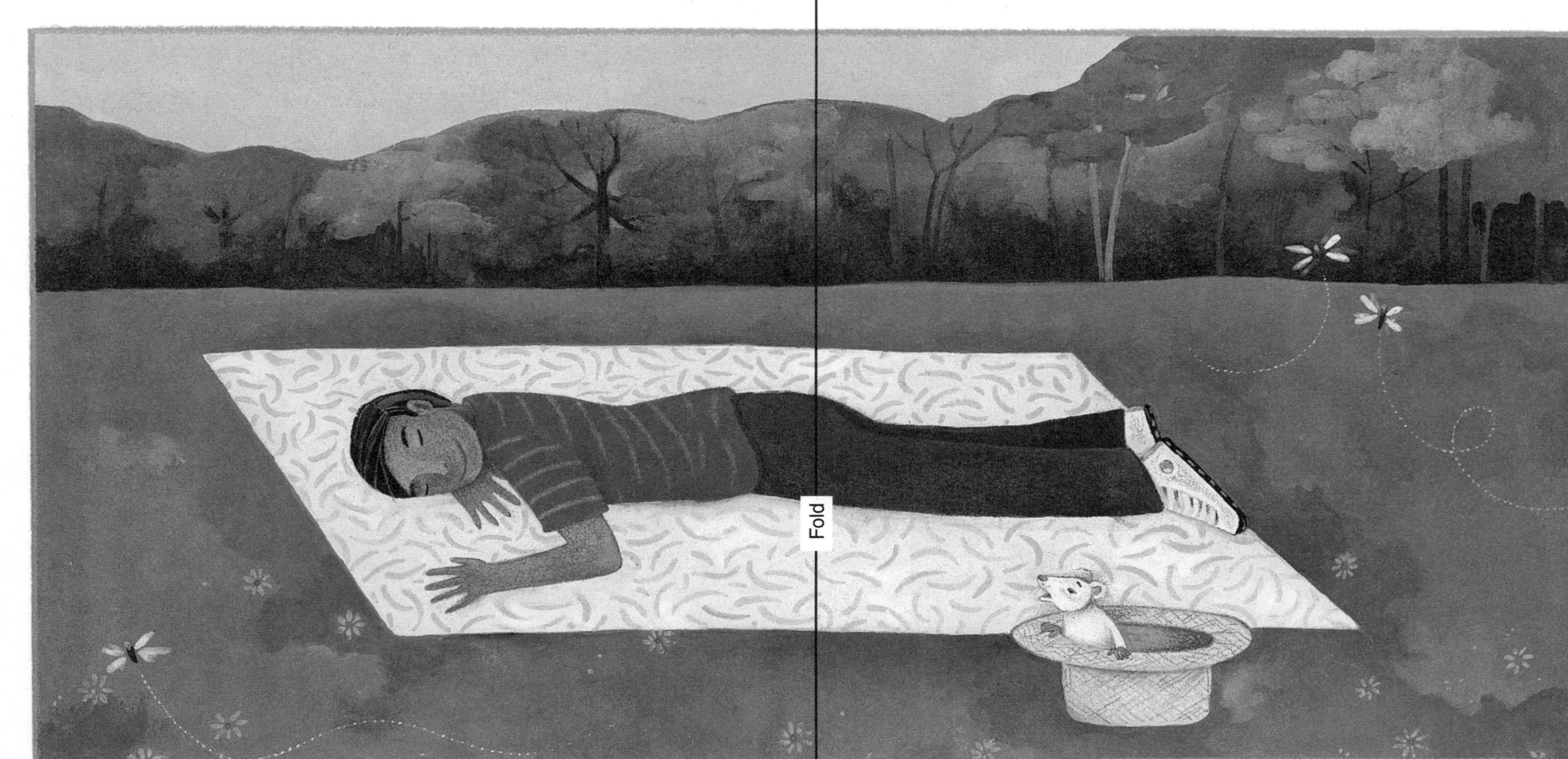

Tim has his nap.

Will Pip nap?

DECODABLE BOOK 4
The Sack

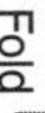

The Sack

by
J.C. Cunningham
illustrated by
Gary Taxali

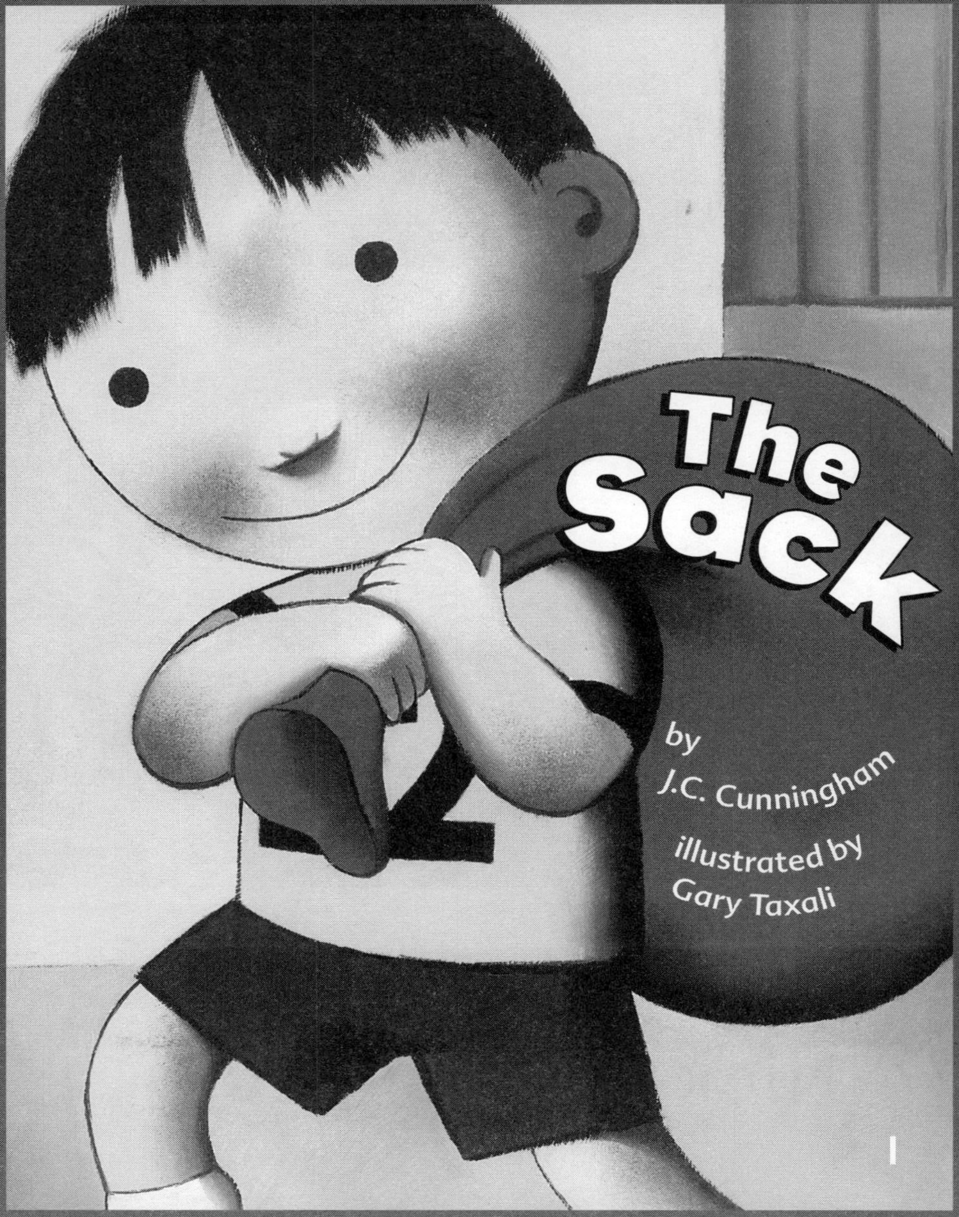

Nick has a sack.

Fold

Fold

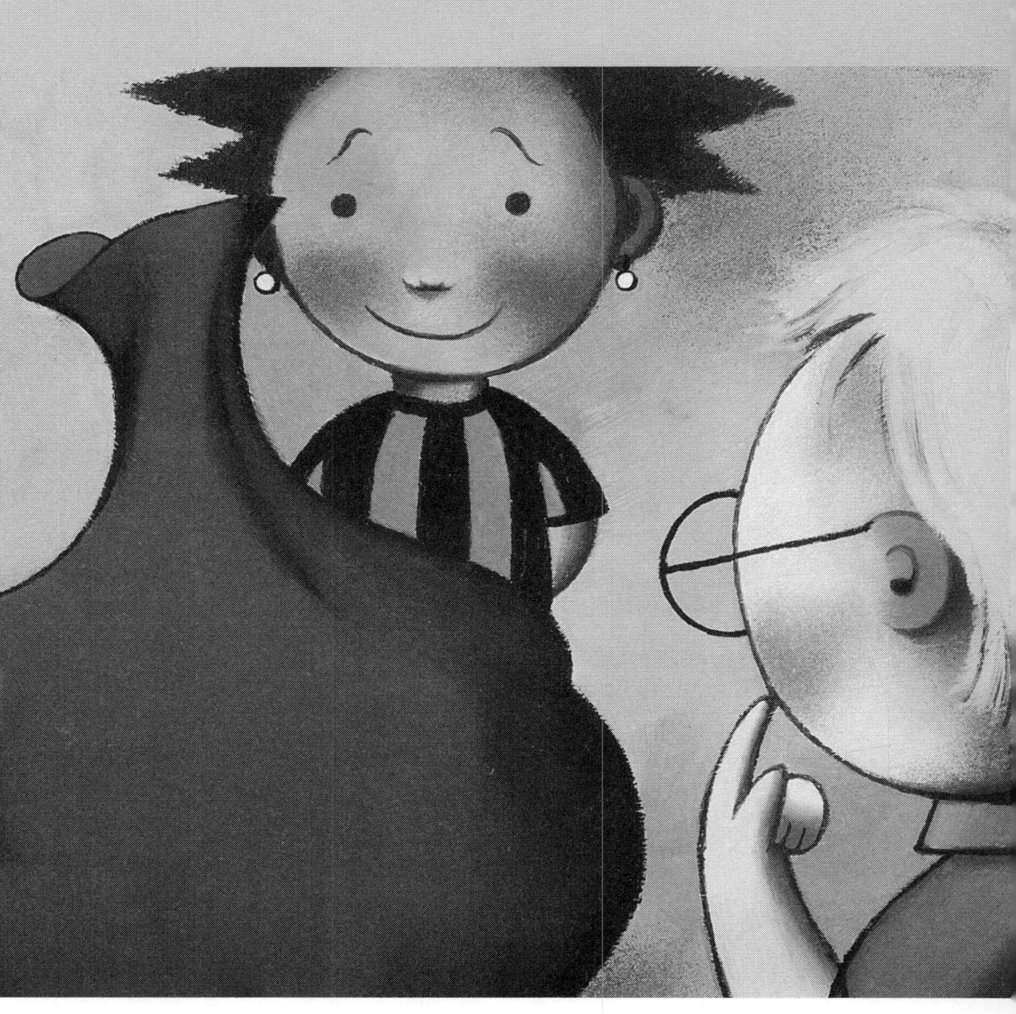

What did Nick pack in his sack?

Is it a cat?
Is it a hat?

Fold

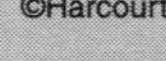

The Sack

Word Count: 49

High-Frequency Words

look
the
what
what's

Decodable Words*

a
can
cat
did
has
hat
his
I
in
is
it
kick
mmmm
Nick
pack
pick
sack

*Words with /k/*ck* appear in **boldface** type.

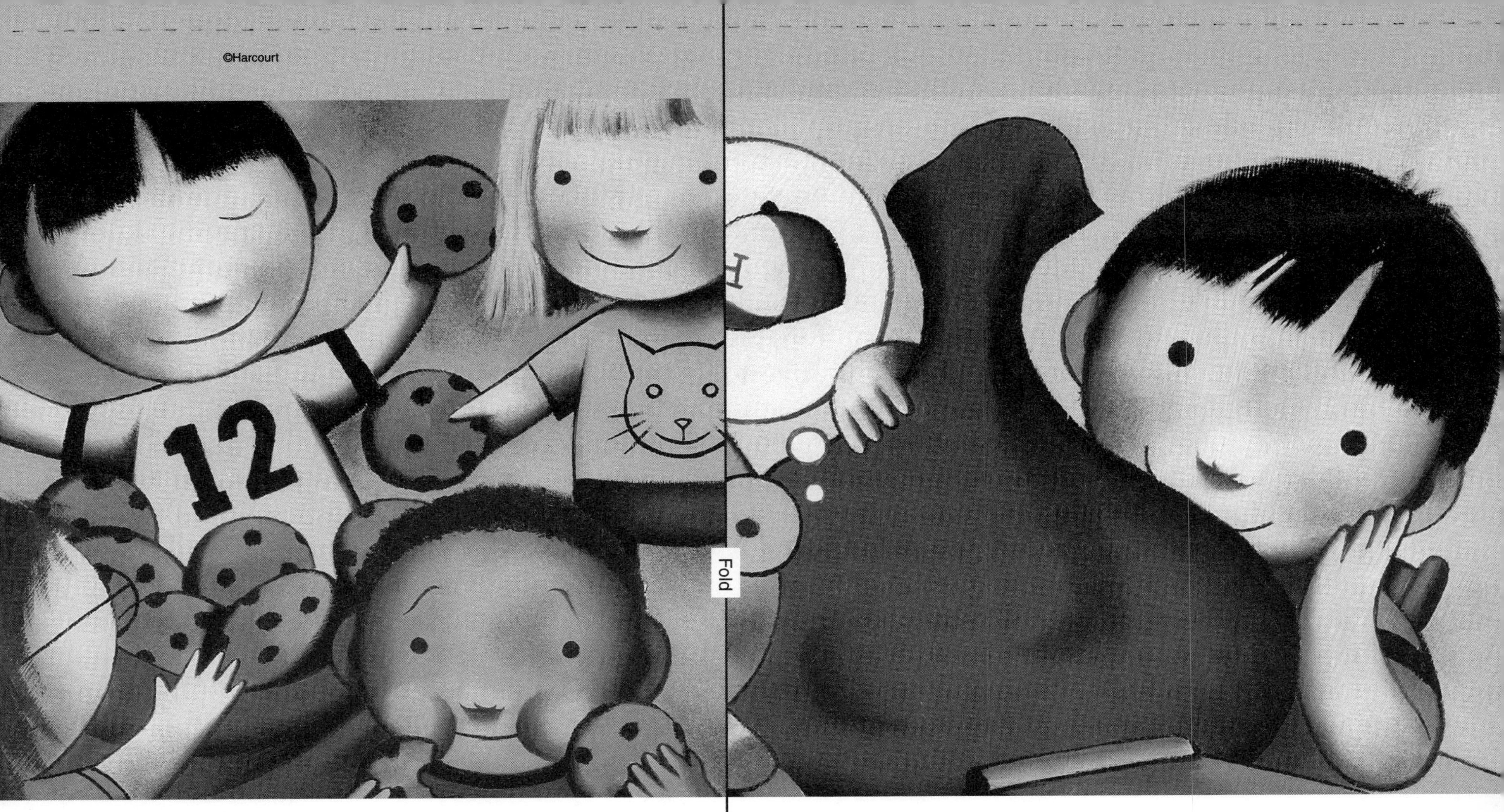

Look what's in
the sack! Mmmm!

What did Nick pack
in his sack?

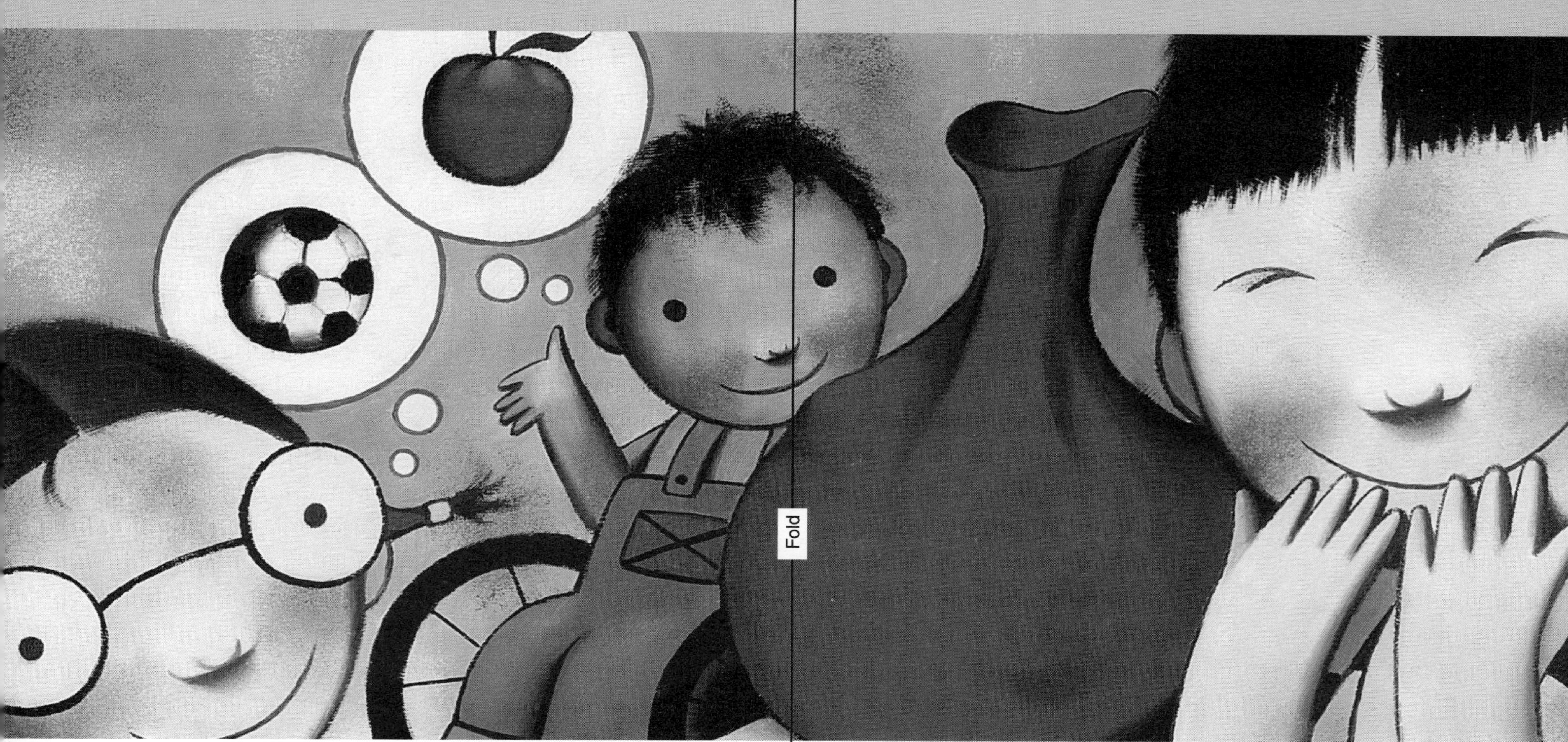

Fold

Can I kick it?
Can I pick it?

What did Nick pack
in his sack?

DECODABLE BOOK 4
Pack the Van

Fold

Pack the Van

by Rose Fabian
illustrated by Dennis Hockerman

Rick! Pack the
mitts in a sack.

Fold

Fold

Nick can help.

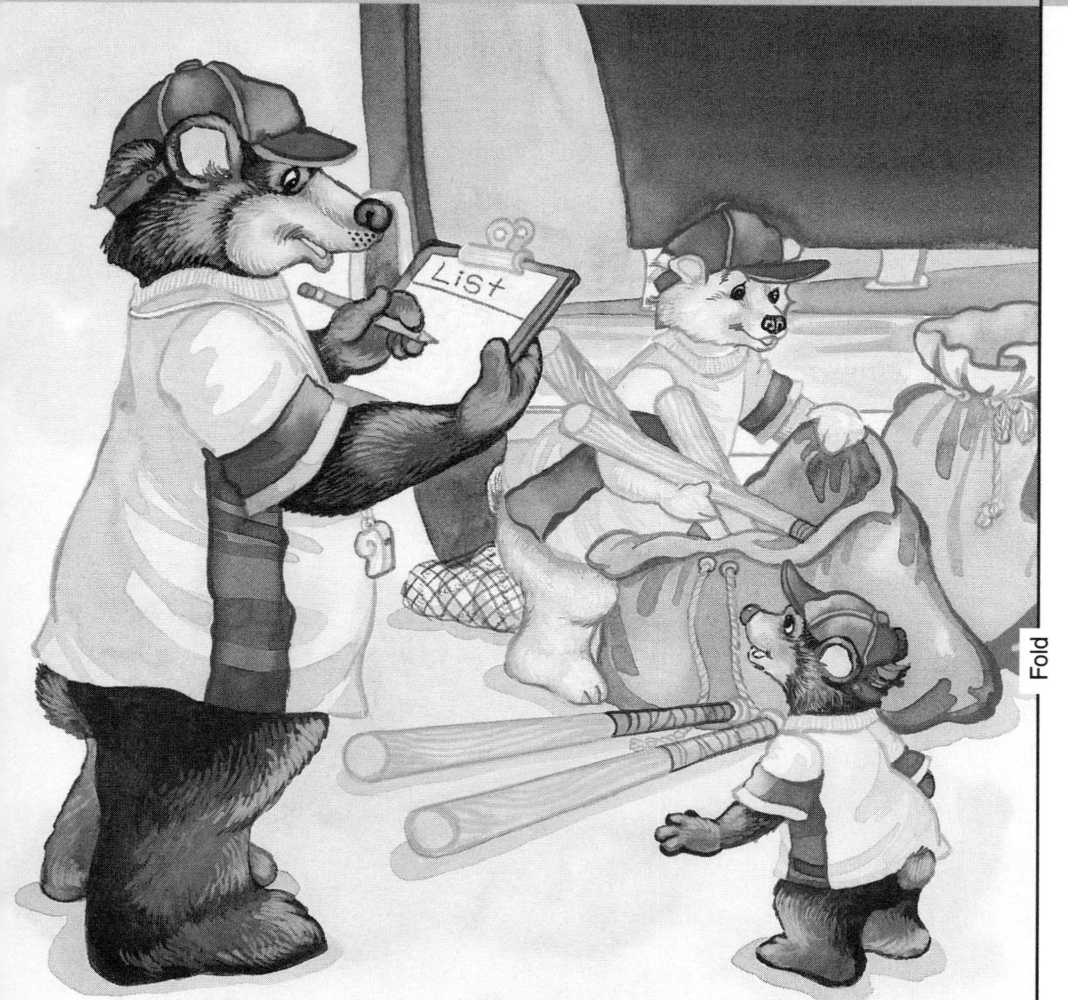

Mack! Pack the bats in a sack.

Fold

Pack the Van

Word Count: 41

High-Frequency Words

come
help
the
up

Decodable Words*

a
back
bats
can
in
Jack
Mack
Mick
mitts
Nick
pack
pick
Rick
sack
van

*Words with /k/*ck* appear in **boldface** type.

Nick can help!

Fold

Nick can help.

Mick! Pick up a sack.
Nick can help.

Fold

Jack! Back up.
Come back, back,
back.

DECODABLE BOOK 5
Todd Fox

Fold

Todd Fox

by Agatha Janes
illustrations by Robert Alan Soulé

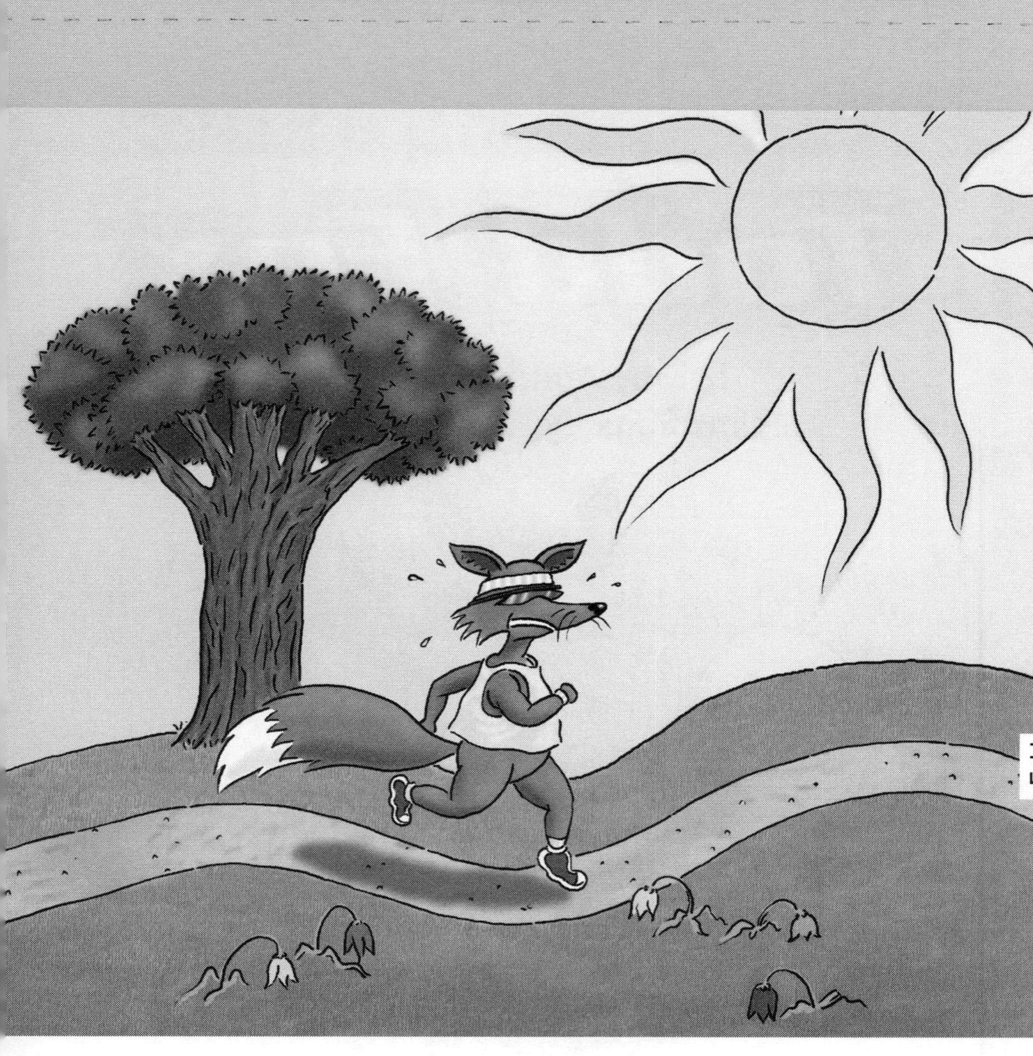

Todd Fox likes to jog.

Fold

Fold

Todd is hot.

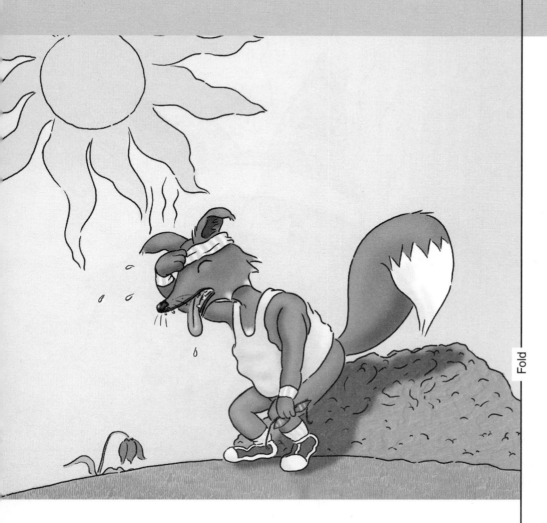

Todd Fox sits
on a rock.

Fold

Todd Fox

Word Count: 47

High-Frequency Words

likes
now
the
to

Decodable Words*

a
and
Fox
hops
hot
is
jog
jogs
log
not
off
on
pond
rock
sits
Todd

*Words with /o/*o* appear in **boldface** type.

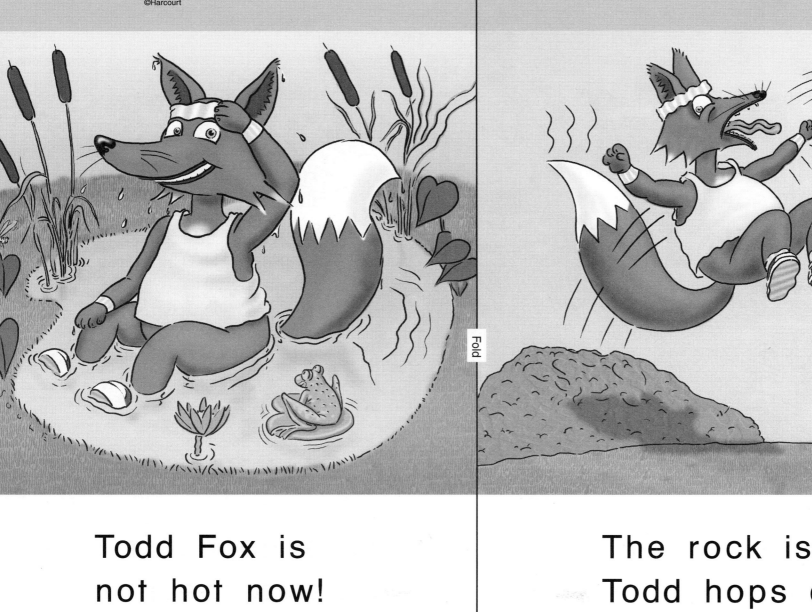

Todd Fox is
not hot now!

Fold

The rock is hot!
Todd hops off.

Todd Fox sits on a log. The log is hot!

Todd hops off and jogs to the pond.

DECODABLE BOOK 5
Dot & Pom-Pom

Fold

Dot and Pom-Pom

by Suzanne Weyn
illustrated by Wallace Keller

Dot is sick.
Pom-Pom is not!

Fold

Pom-Pom hops up.
Dot can not nap.

Fold

Pom-Pom hops on Dot!
Dot can not nap.

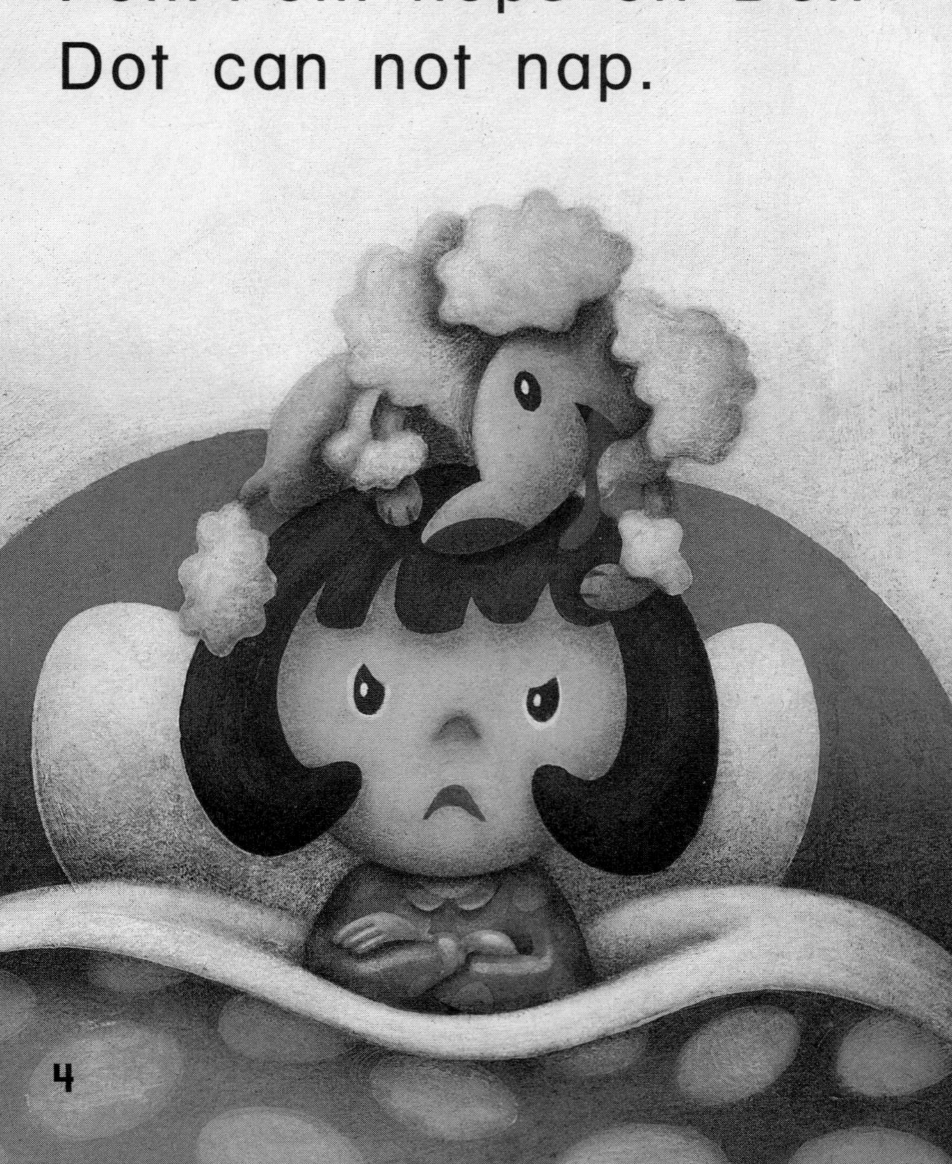

Fold

Dot and Pom-Pom

Word Count: 50

High-Frequency Words

look
up

Decodable Words*

a
and
at
can
Dot
Dot's
hops
is
last
nap
not
on
Pom-Pom
pot
sick
sock
tips

*Words with /o/*o* appear in **boldface** type.

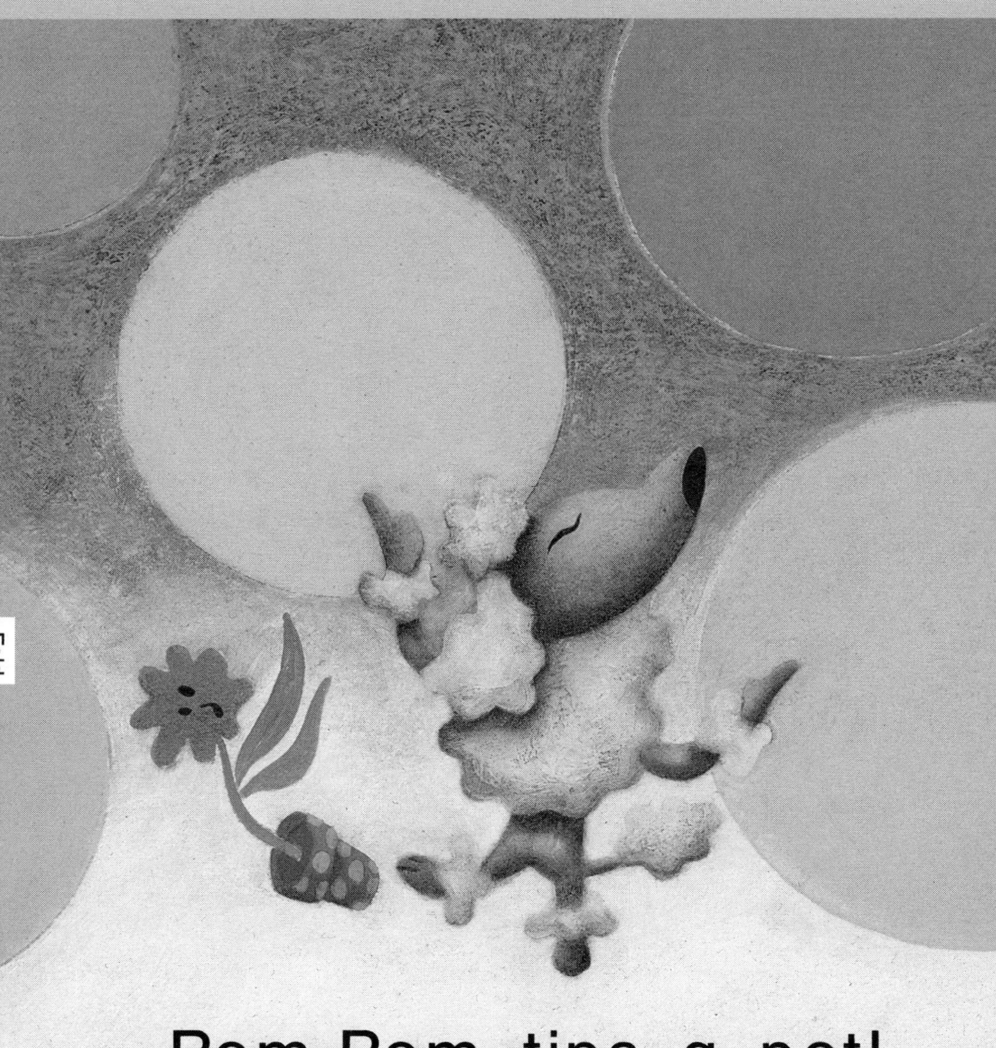

At last, Dot can nap.

Fold

Pom-Pom tips a pot!
Dot can not nap.

Fold

Look at Dot's sock!
Dot can not nap.

DECODABLE BOOK 6
At the Mall

Fold

At the Mall

by
Della Rowland

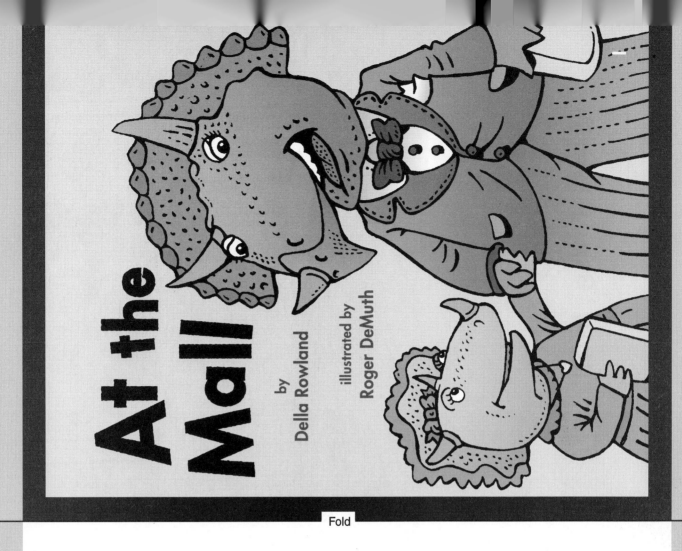

illustrated by
Roger DeMuth

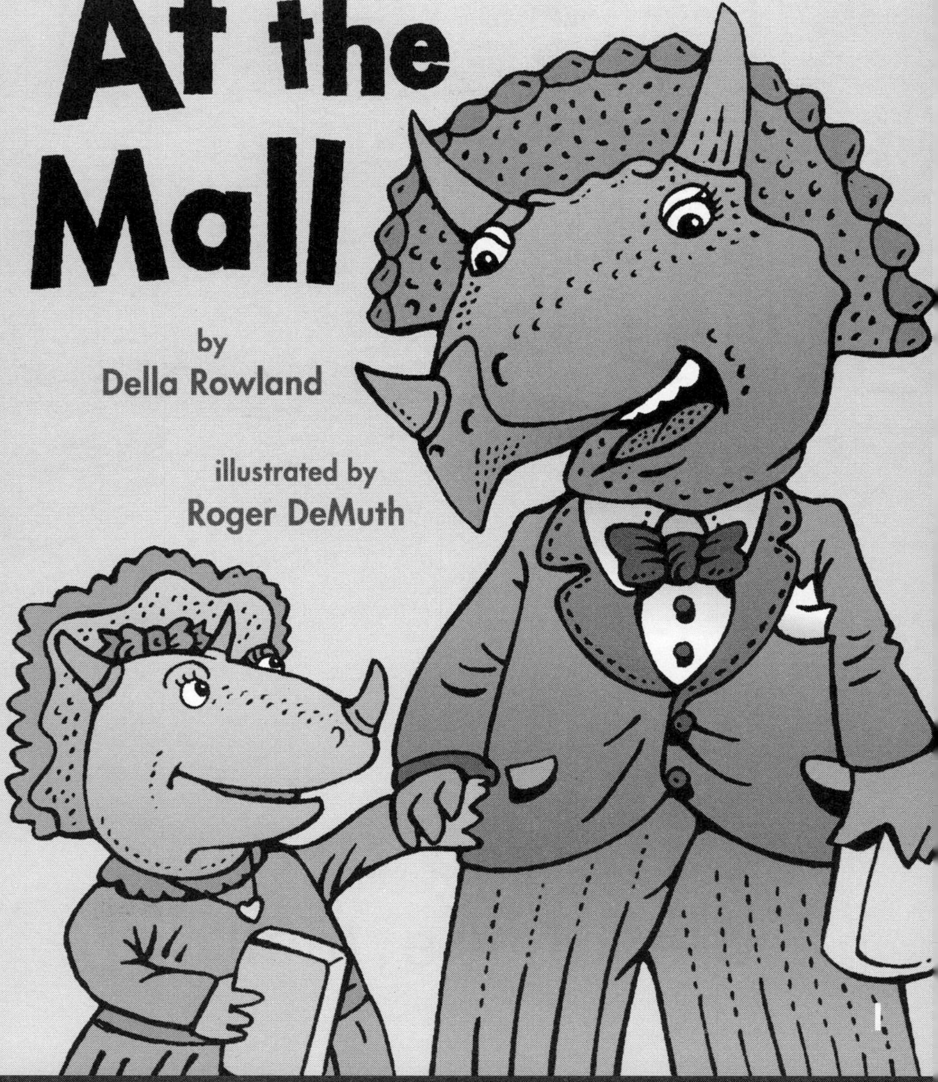

Cass and Dad
are at the mall.

Fold

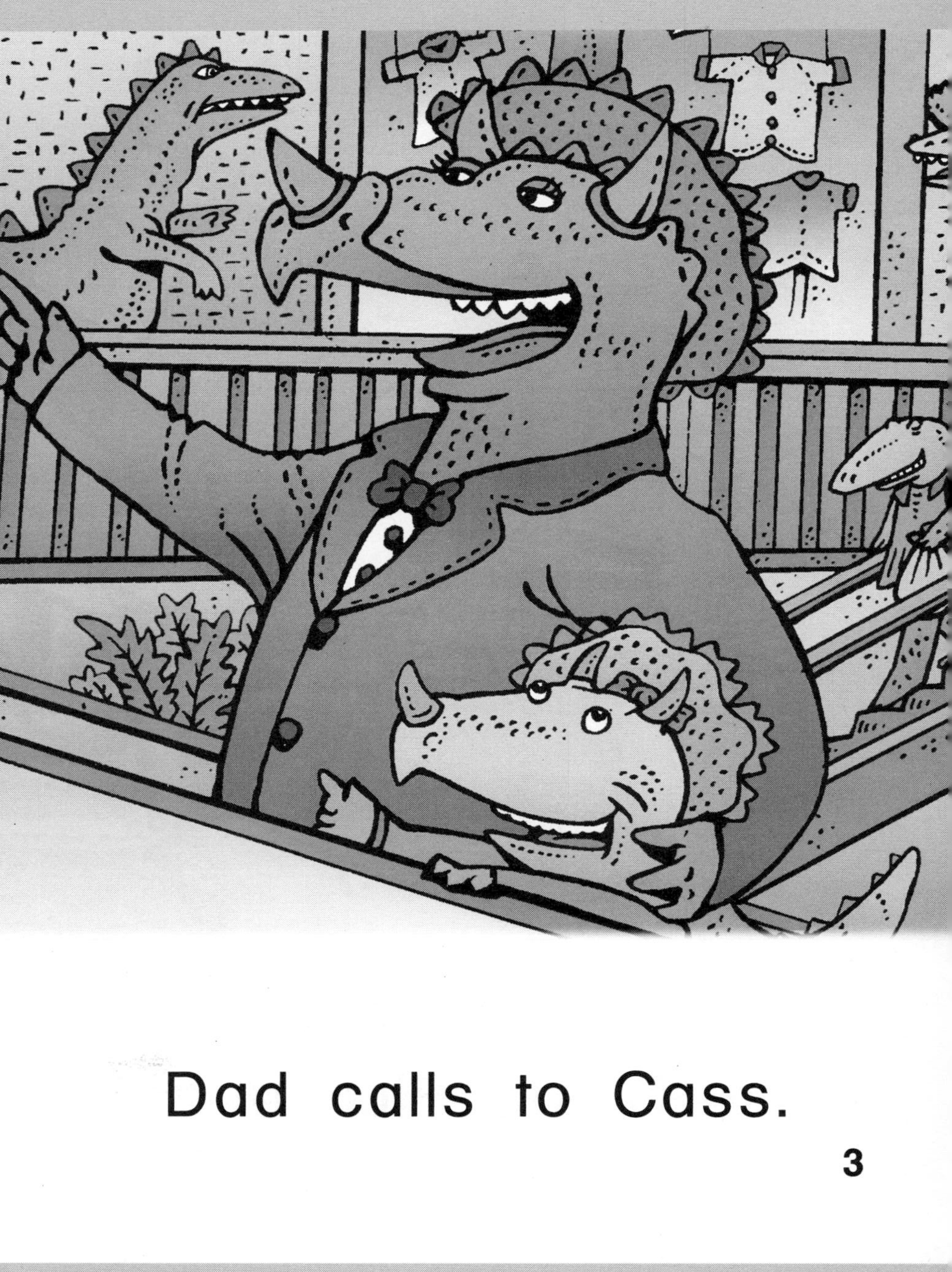

Fold

Dad calls to Cass.

Look at all the caps!
Pick, Cass. Pick a cap.

Fold

At the Mall

Word Count: 49

High-Frequency Words

are
look
now
the
to
too

Decodable Words*

a
all
and
at
calls
can
cap
caps
Cass
Dad
is
mall
nap
pick
picked
picks
sad
small
tall

*Words with /ô/*a* appear in **boldface** type.

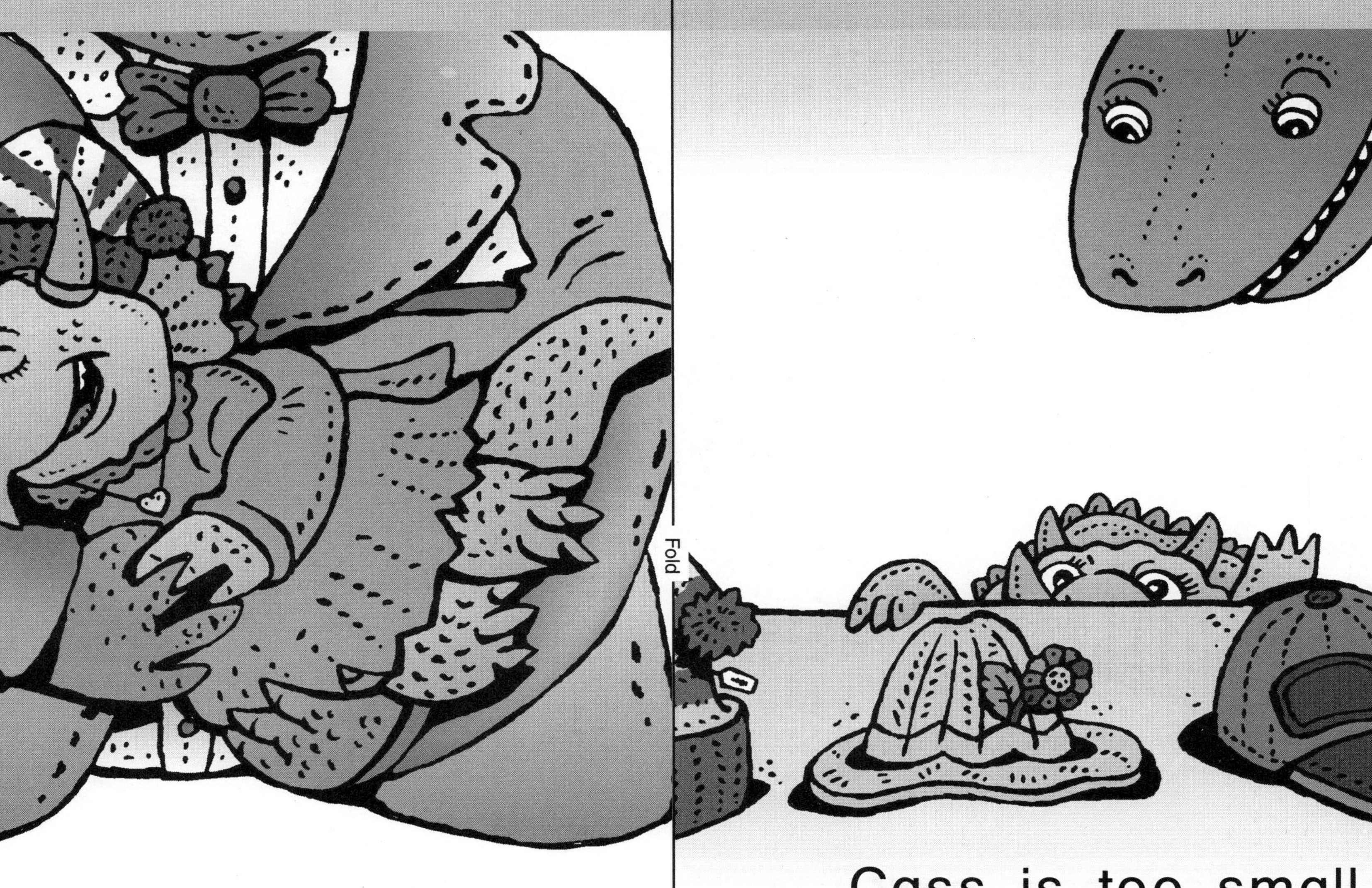

Cass picked a nap cap!

Fold

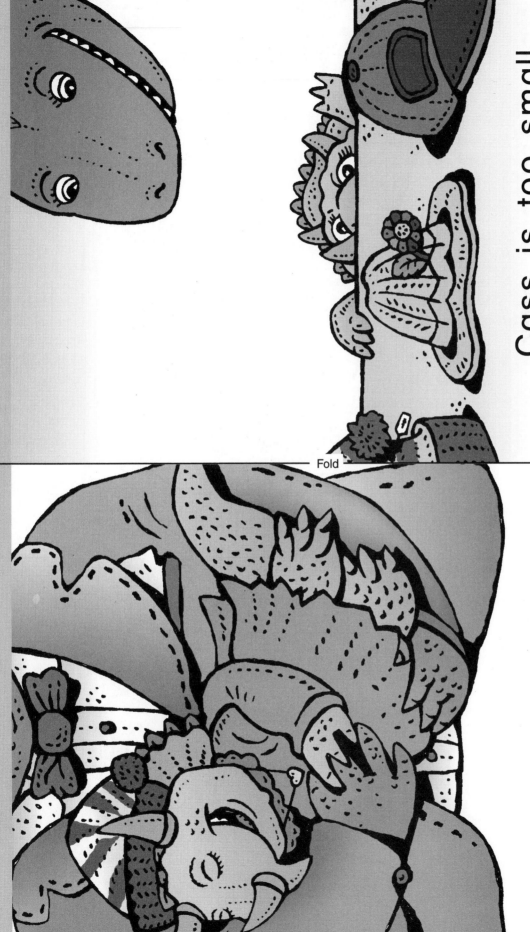

Cass is too small.
Cass is sad.

Fold

Now Cass can pick.
Cass is tall, tall, tall!

Cass picks a cap.

DECODABLE BOOK 6
Tall, Small, Tall

Fold

Tall, Small, Tall

by Petra Ortmann

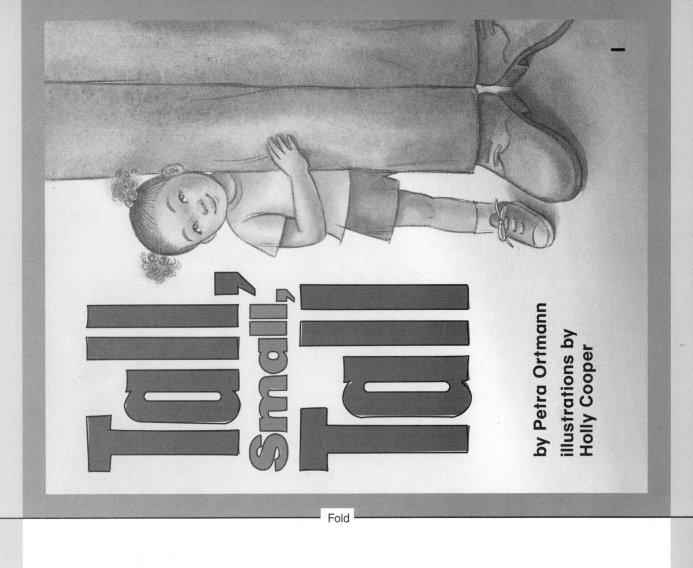

illustrations by Holly Cooper

Dad is tall.

Fold

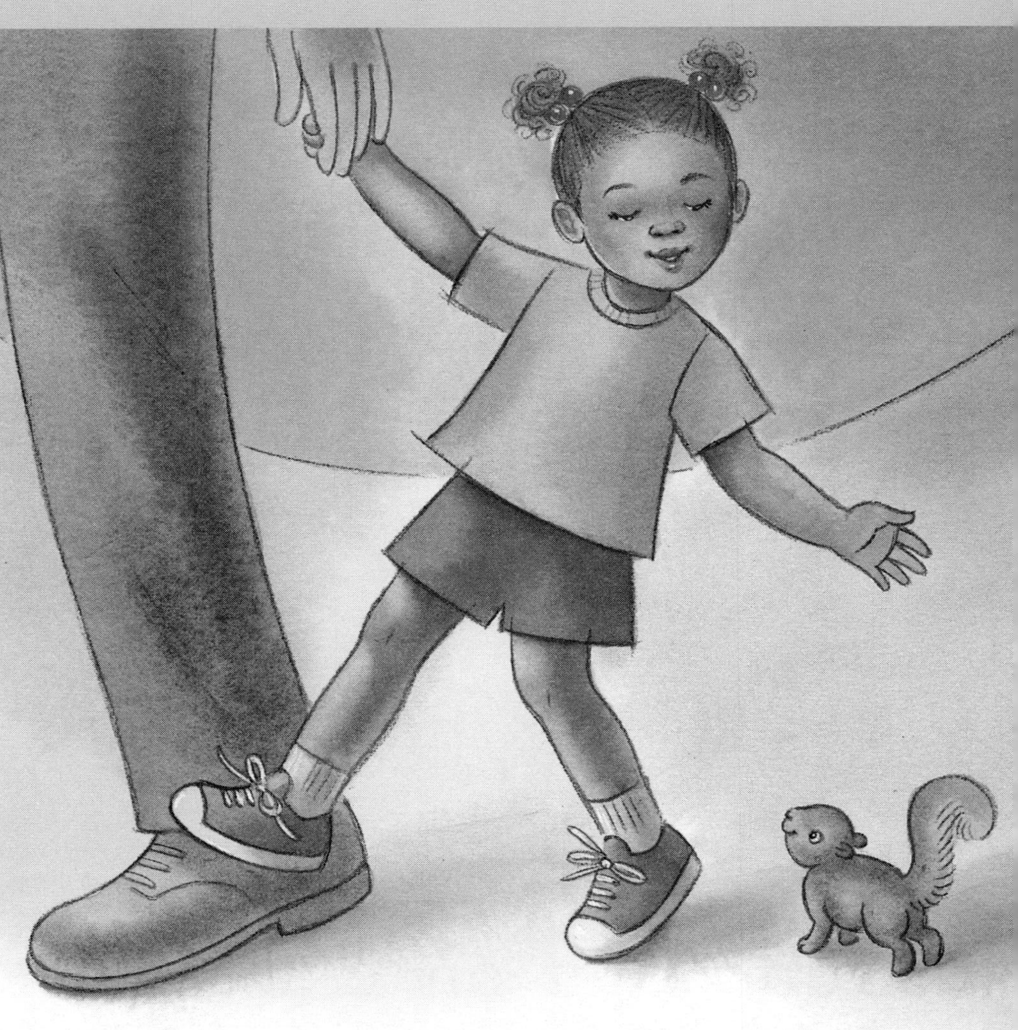

Kim is not tall at all.
Kim is small.

Fold

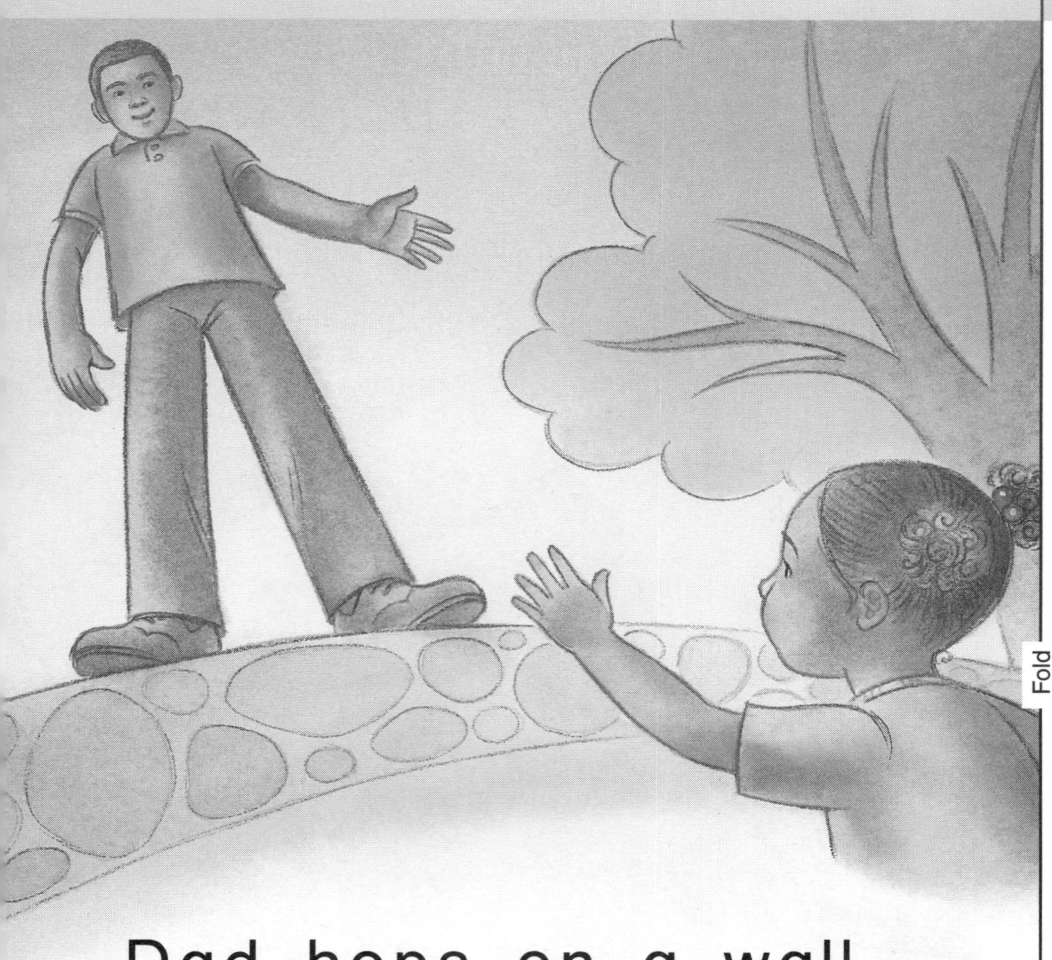

Dad hops on a wall.
Now Dad is tall,
tall, tall!

Fold

Tall, Small, Tall

Word Count: 54

High-Frequency Words

helps
now
the

Decodable Words*

a
all
at
Dad
fall
hop
hops
is
Kim
not
off
on
small
tall
wall
will

*Words with /ô/*a* appear in **boldface** type.

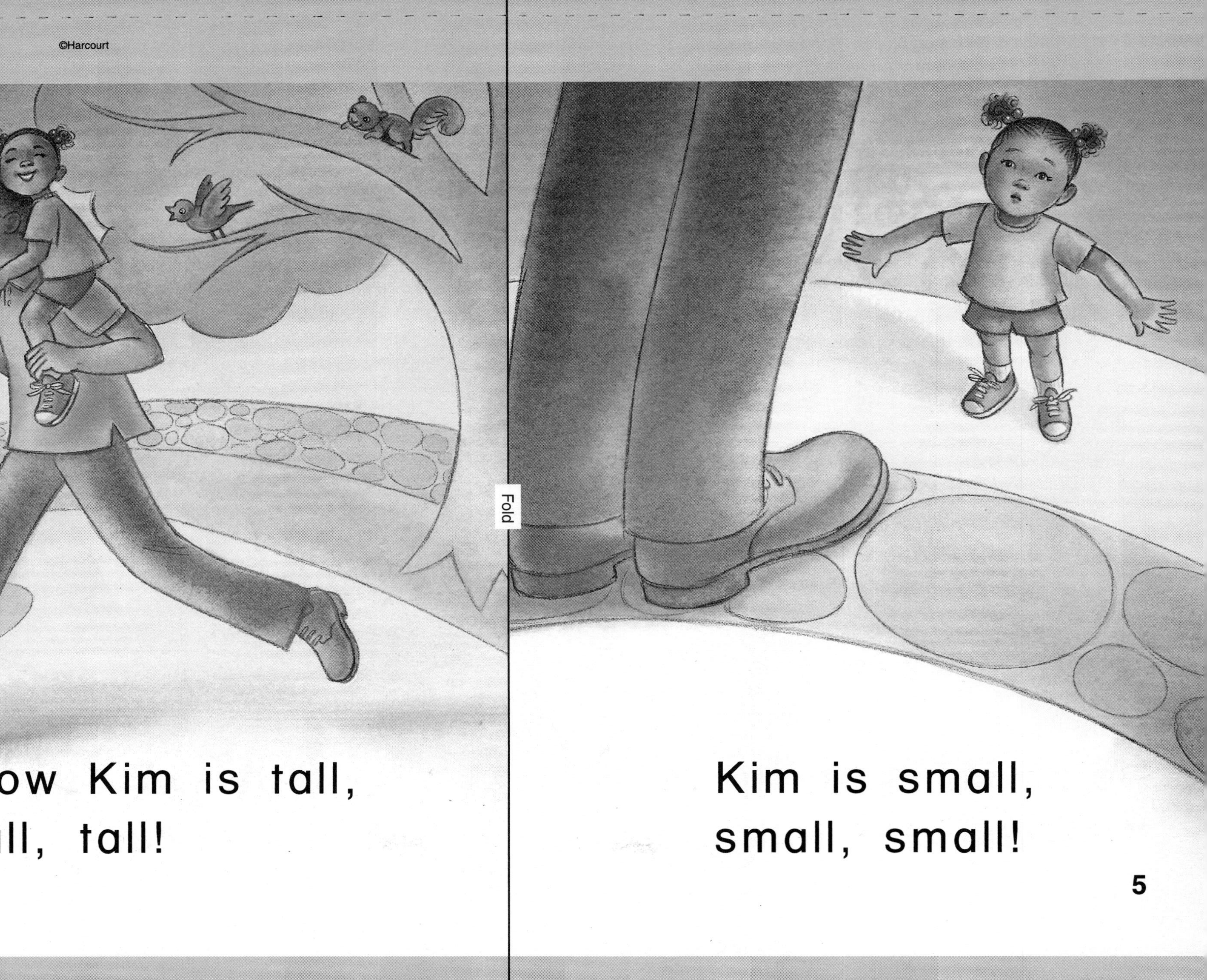

Now Kim is tall,
tall, tall!

Kim is small,
small, small!

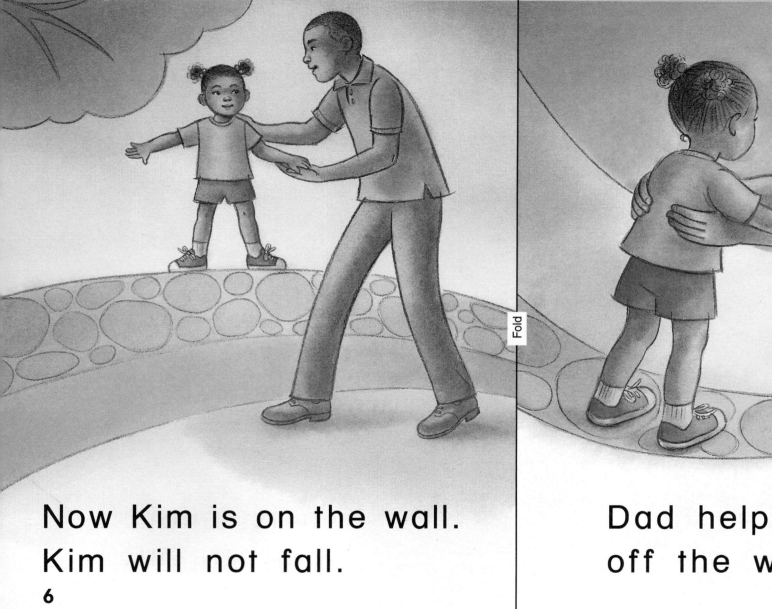

Fold

Now Kim is on the wall.
Kim will not fall.

Dad helps Kim hop
off the wall.

DECODABLE BOOK 7
Ben & Bell

Fold

Ben and Bell

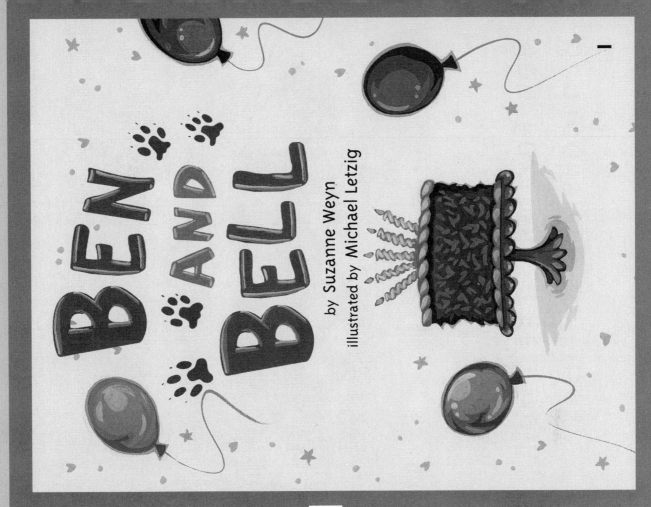

by Suzanne Weyn
illustrated by Michael Letzig

Ben Fox gets a red doll.
Ben calls his doll Bell.

Fold

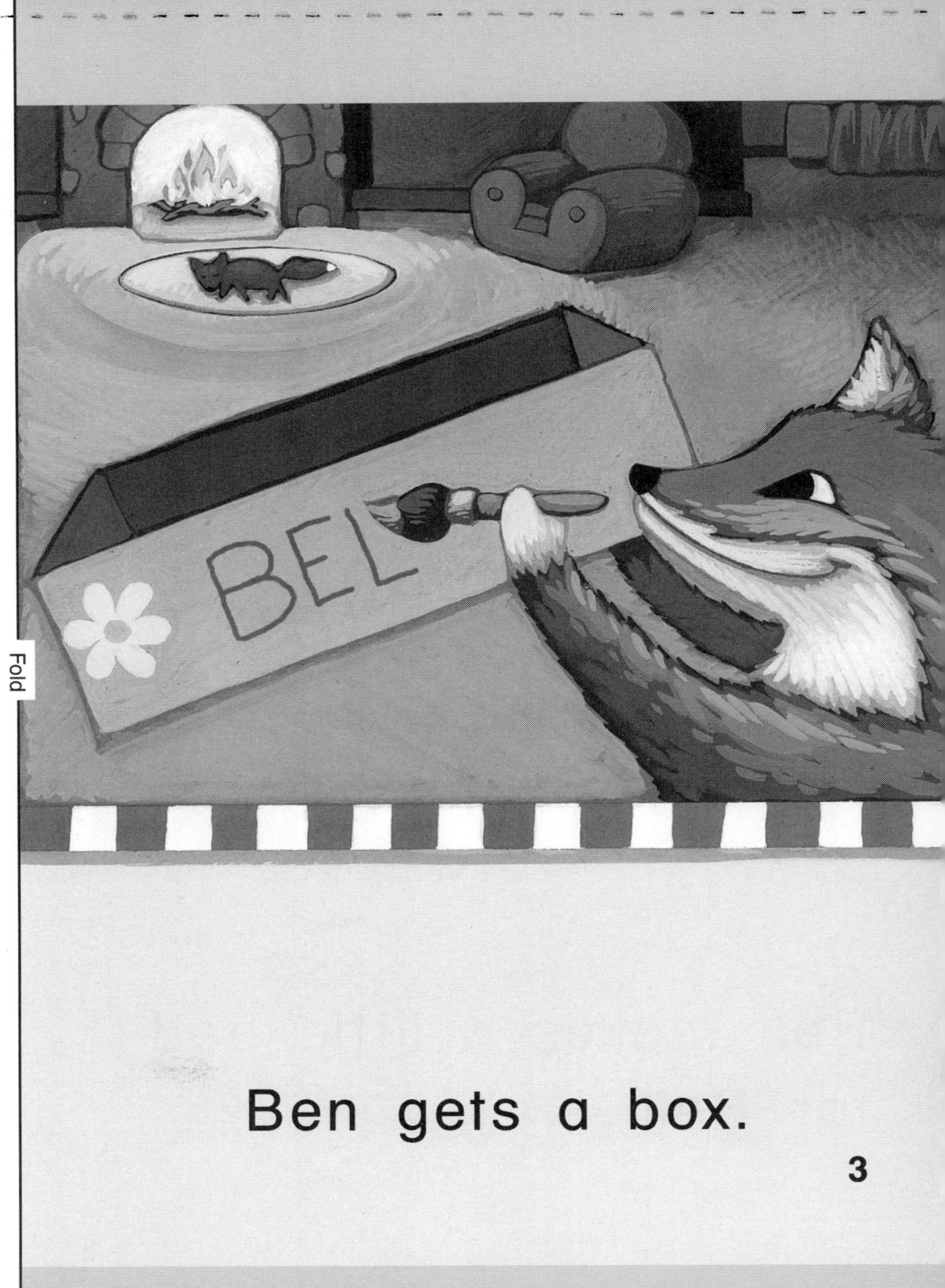

Ben gets a box.

Fold

Ben makes a little bed
for Bell.

Fold

Ben and Bell

Word Count: 68

High-Frequency Words

for
little
makes
now
that
the
too

Decodable Words*

a
and
bed
Bell
Ben
best
big
box
calls
can
can't
doll
Fox
gets
his
in
is
it
pats
red
rest
rests
tells

*Words with /e/*e* appear in **boldface** type.

Now Ben can rest.
Bell can rest in the
big bed, too!

Fold

Ben tells Bell that it is
the best bed for a doll.

Ben pats his doll.
Bell rests in the
little bed.

Fold

Ben gets in his big bed.
Ben can't rest!

DECODABLE BOOK 7
Red Hen

Fold

Red Hen

by J. C. Cunningham
illustrations by Jason Wolff

Peck, peck, peck.
Ten hens peck
in the pen.

Fold

Red Hen isn't
in the pen.

Fold

Ten hens call to Red.
"Come and peck!"

Fold

Red Hen

Word Count: 65

High-Frequency Words

the
to
come
my
you
look
now
they
me

Decodable Words*

and	**peck**
call	**pen**
can	**Red**
can't	**rest**
hen	**ten**
hens	**well**
I	**yell**
in	**yells**
isn't	**yes**
let	**yet**
nest	
not	

*Words with /e/*e* appear in **boldface** type.

"Yes!" Red yells. "Look!"
"Well, well, well!" ten
hens yell.

Fold

"Not yet," Red yells.
"I can't peck now. Let
me rest in my nest!"

Peck, peck, peck.
Ten hens peck
in the pen.

Fold

"Red!" they call.
"Can you peck now?"

DECODABLE BOOK 8
Seth's Pet

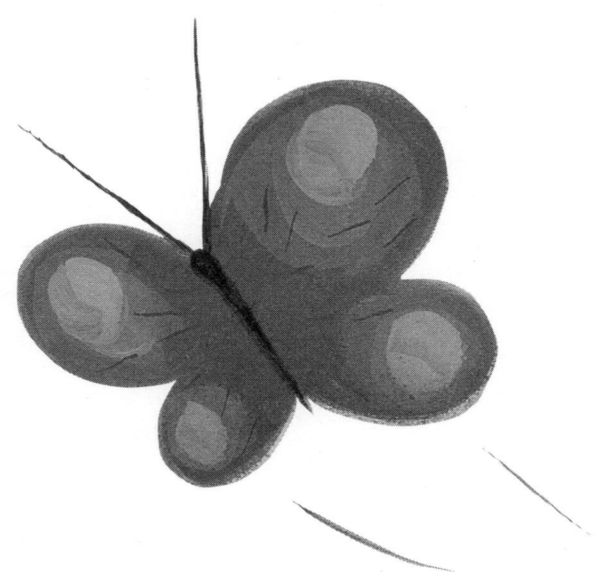

Fold

Seth's Pet

by Amy E. Weingartner
illustrated by Joung Un Kim

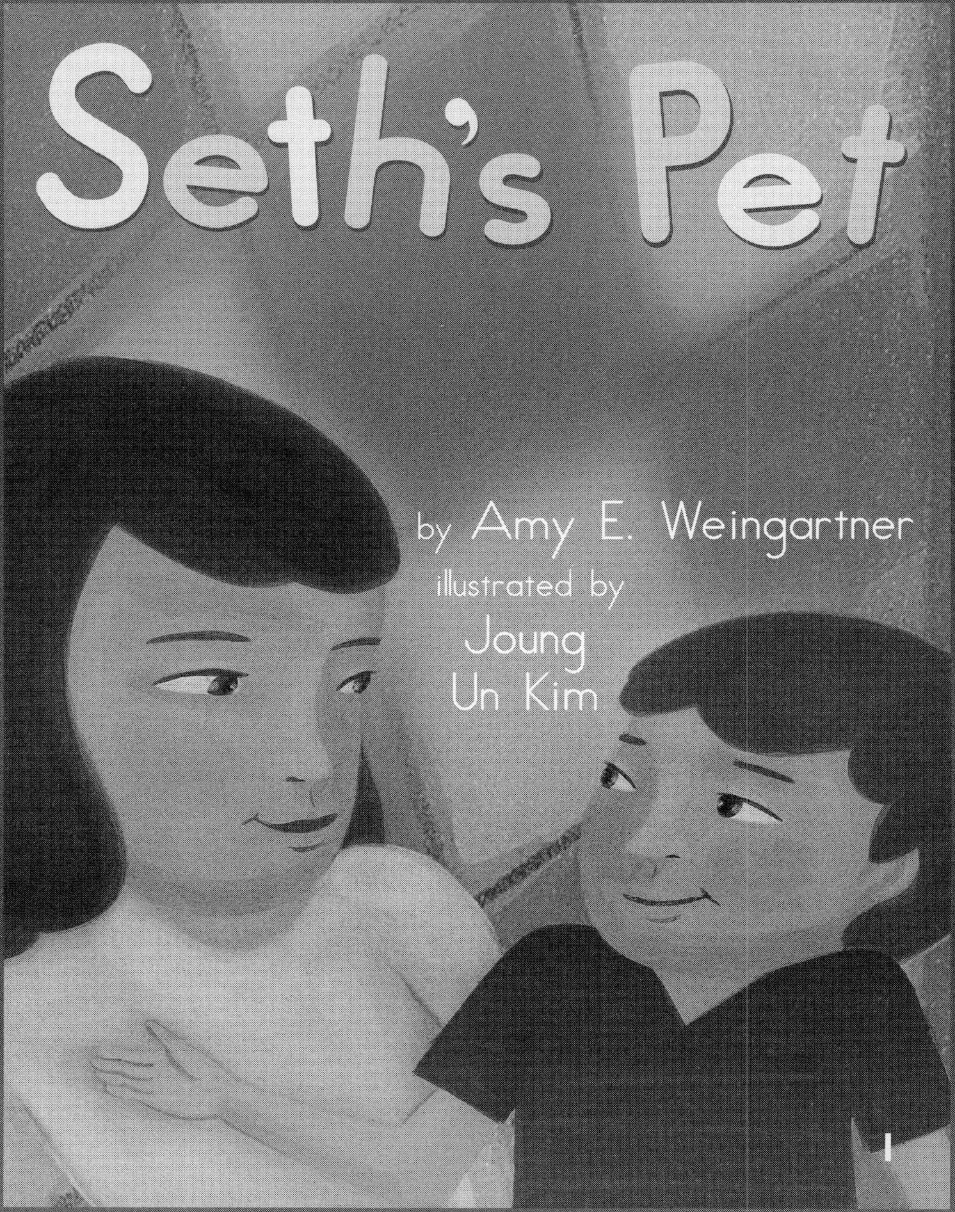

Seth is looking for Hip-Hop.
Mom is with him.

Fold

Hip-Hop isn't on
this mat.
Did Hip-Hop hop down
that path?

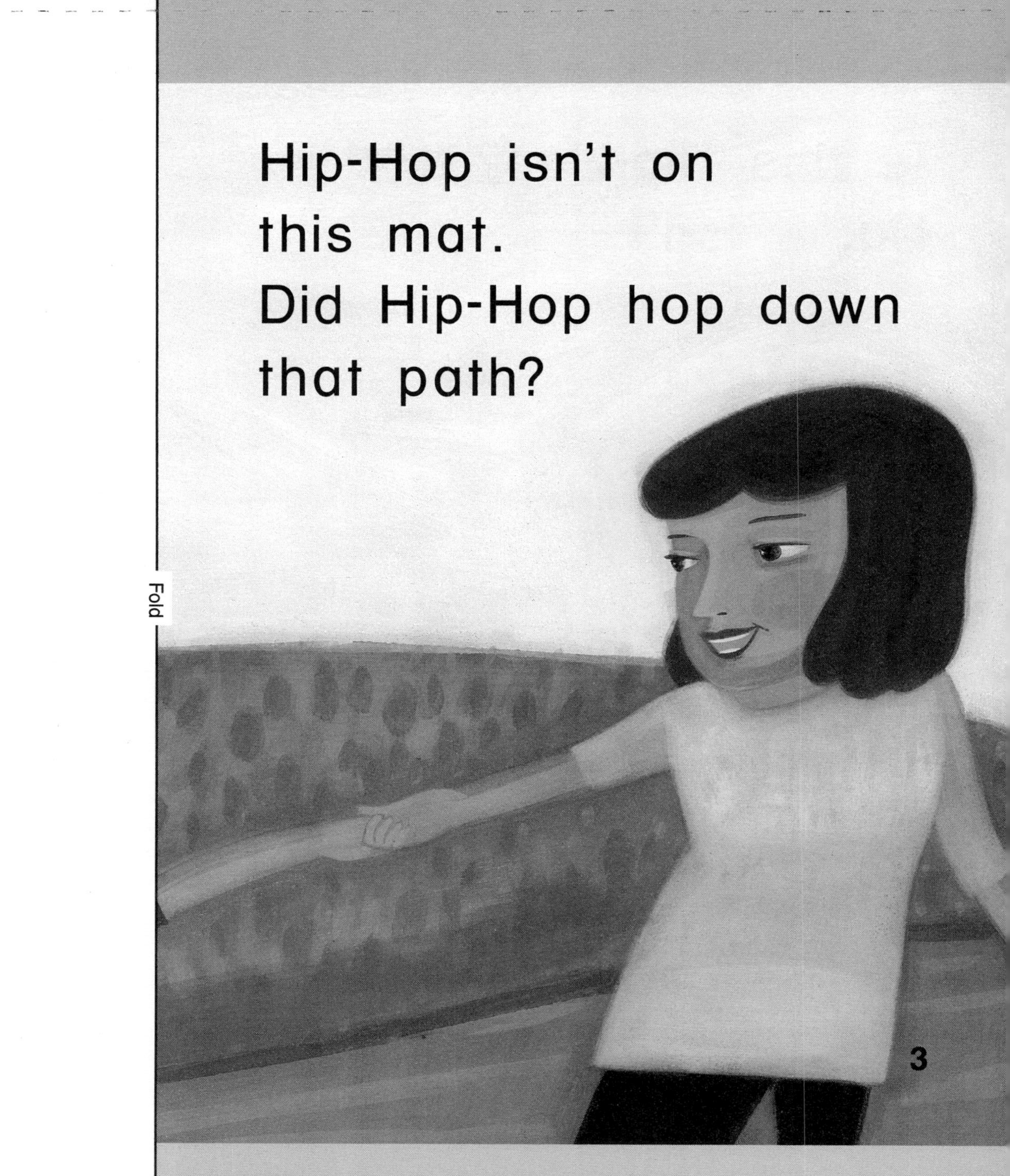

Fold

Is this Hip-Hop?
No, it isn't.

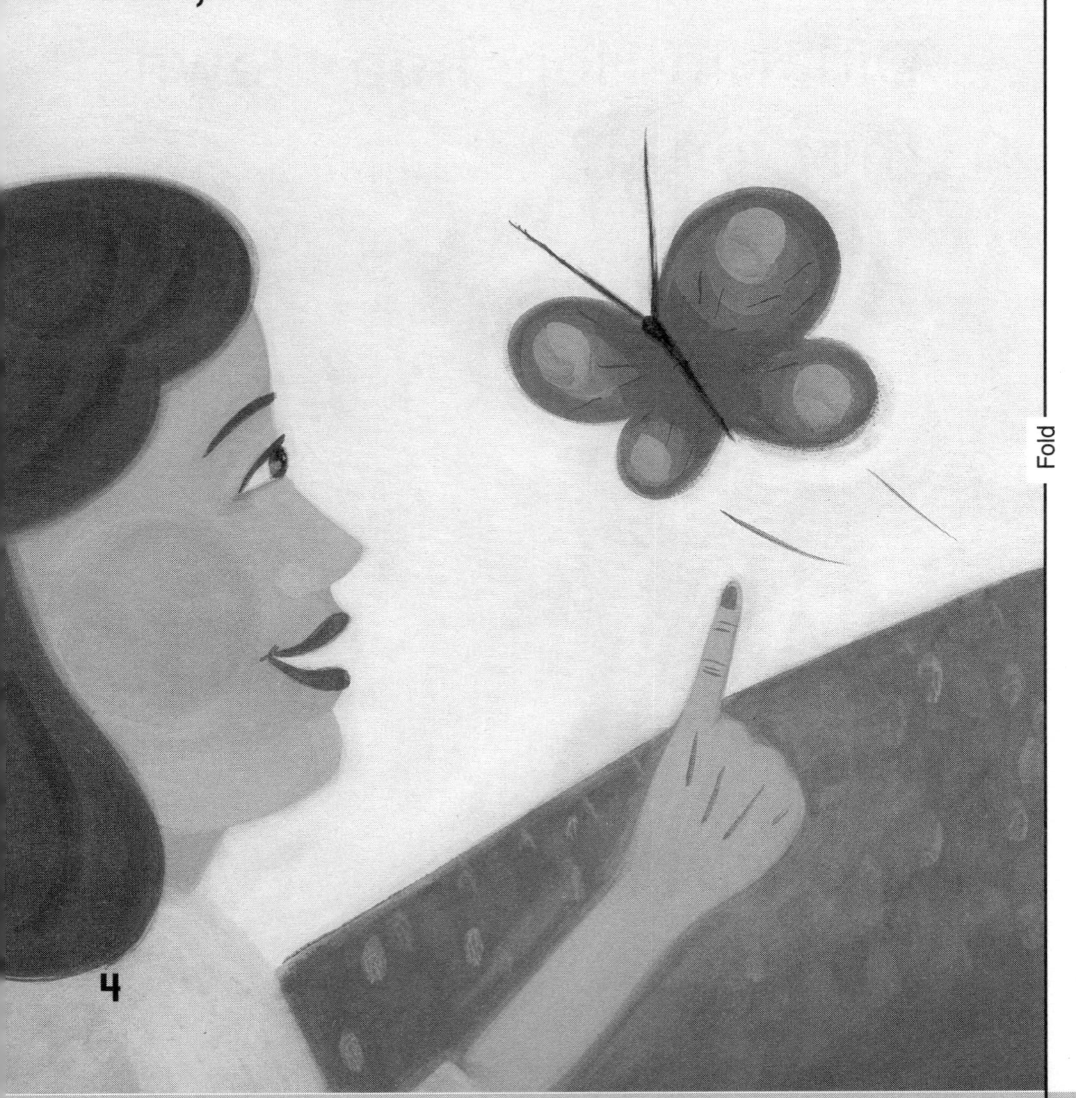

Fold

Seth's Pet

Word Count: 63

High-Frequency Words

down
for
look
looking
no
see

Decodable Words*

did
him
Hip-Hop
hop
is
isn't
it
it's
mat
Mom
on
path
pet
Seth
Seth's
tells
thanks
that
then
think
this
with
yes

*Words with /th/*th* appear in **boldface** type.

Yes, it is! It's Hip-Hop!
"Thanks, Mom!"

Fold

Hop, hop, hop.
Is that Hip-Hop? No.

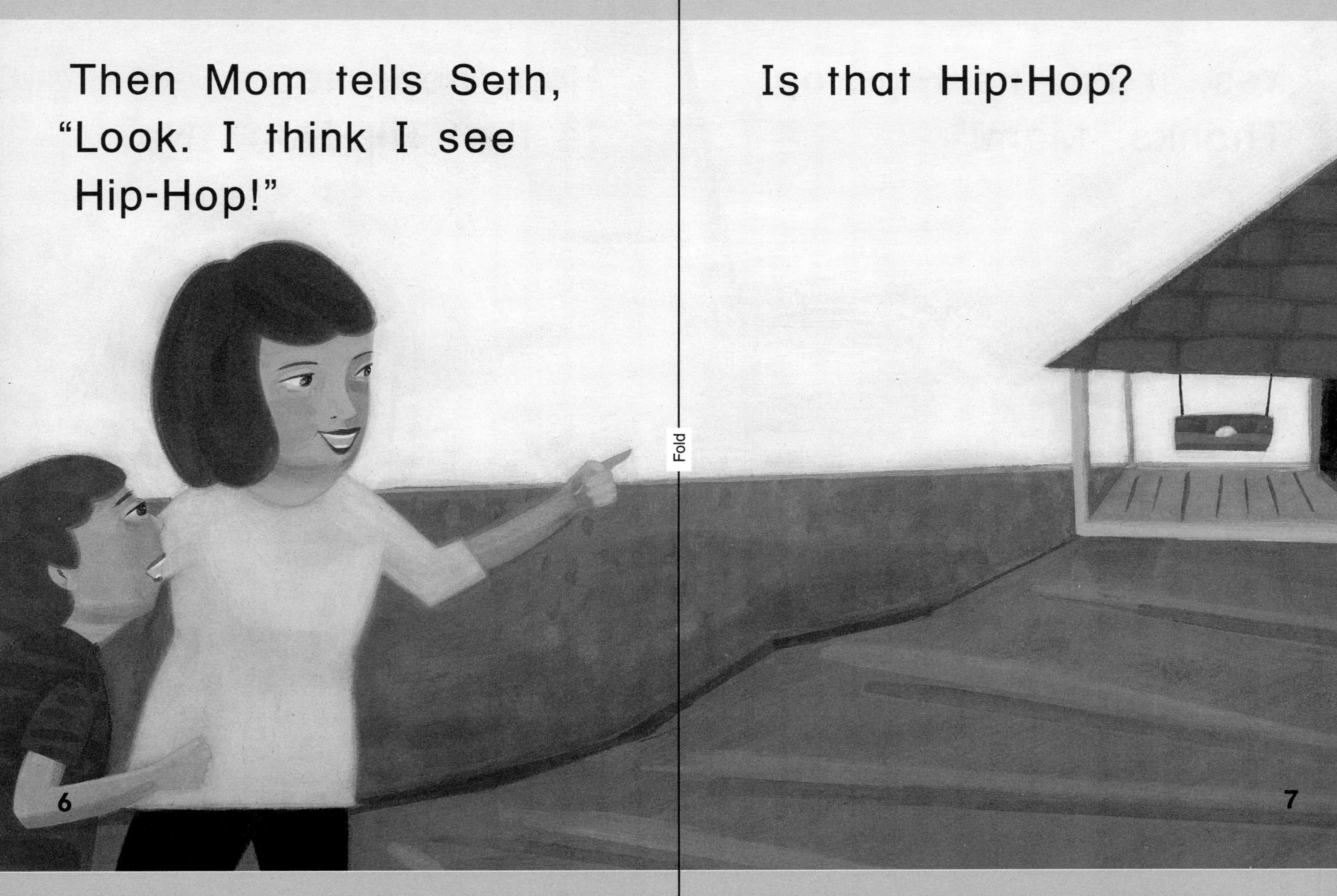

Then Mom tells Seth,
"Look. I think I see
Hip-Hop!"

Is that Hip-Hop?

Fold

DECODABLE BOOK 8
Math Path

Fold

Math Path

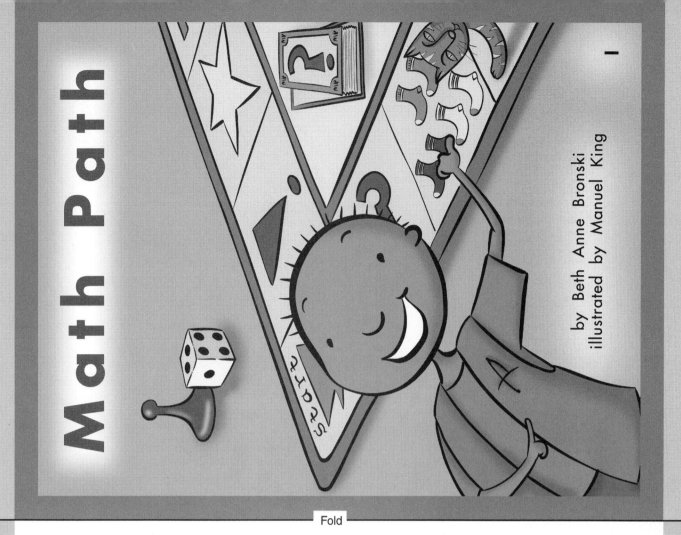

by Beth Anne Bronski
illustrated by Manuel King

This is the math path.
Add and think!

Fold

Fold

Add 2 socks and
4 socks.
What did you get?

Did you get 6?
Then you are on
the math path!

Fold

Math Path

Word Count: 79

High-Frequency Words

see
the
what
you
are

Decodable Words*

add
and
cats
did
fat
get
is
math
on
path
pens
pins
socks
them
then
thin
think
this
with

*Words with /th/*th* appear in **boldface** type.

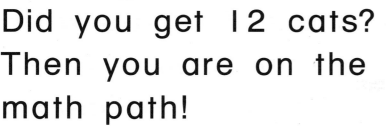

Did you get 12 cats?
Then you are on the
math path!

Fold

See 5 pens with 5 pins.
Add them. Think!
What did you get?

Did you get 10?
Then you are on
the math path!

Fold

Add 6 fat cats with
6 thin cats.
What did you get?

DECODABLE BOOK 9
Muff's Bath

Fold

Muff's Bath

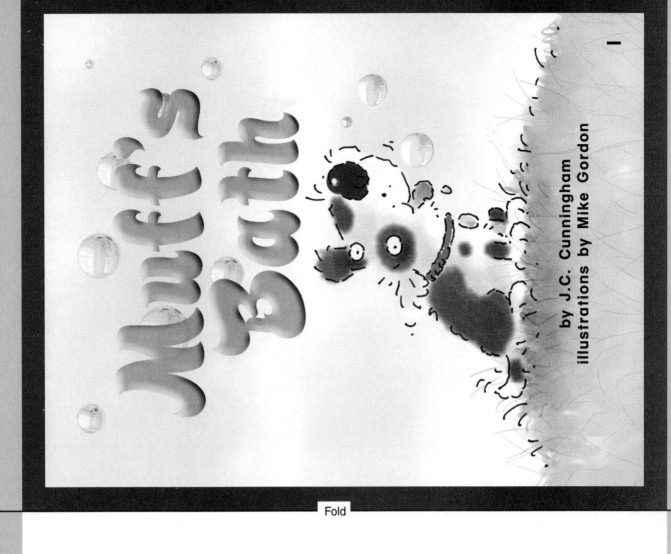

by J.C. Cunningham
illustrations by Mike Gordon

Muff is Bud’s new pup.
Muff runs and jumps.

Fold

Fold

Muff runs and jumps in the mud! Muff must get a bath.

Bud fills a tub
with suds.
"Jump in, Muff!"

Fold

Muff's Bath

Word Count: 74

High-Frequency Words

are
likes
new
see
the
too
you'll

Decodable Words*

a	**huff**	on
and	**hugs**	**puff**
at	in	**pup**
bath	is	**rubs**
baths	it	**ruff**
Bud	**jump**	**runs**
Bud's	**jumps**	**suds**
but	**mud**	**tub**
fills	**Muff**	**tugs**
fun	**Muff's**	will
get	**must**	with
gets	not	

*Words with /u/*u* appear in **boldface** type.

Muff gets a bath, but
Bud gets a bath, too!

Fold

Bud tugs at Muff.
Huff! Puff!
Muff will not get
in the tub.

Bud hugs Muff.
"Baths are fun, Muff.
You'll see."

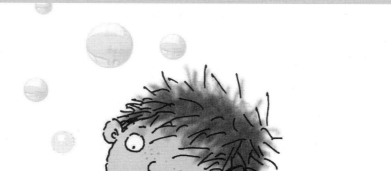

Fold

Bud rubs suds on Muff.
"Ruff! Ruff!"
Muff likes it!

DECODABLE BOOK 9
Buck Duck

Fold

Buck Duck

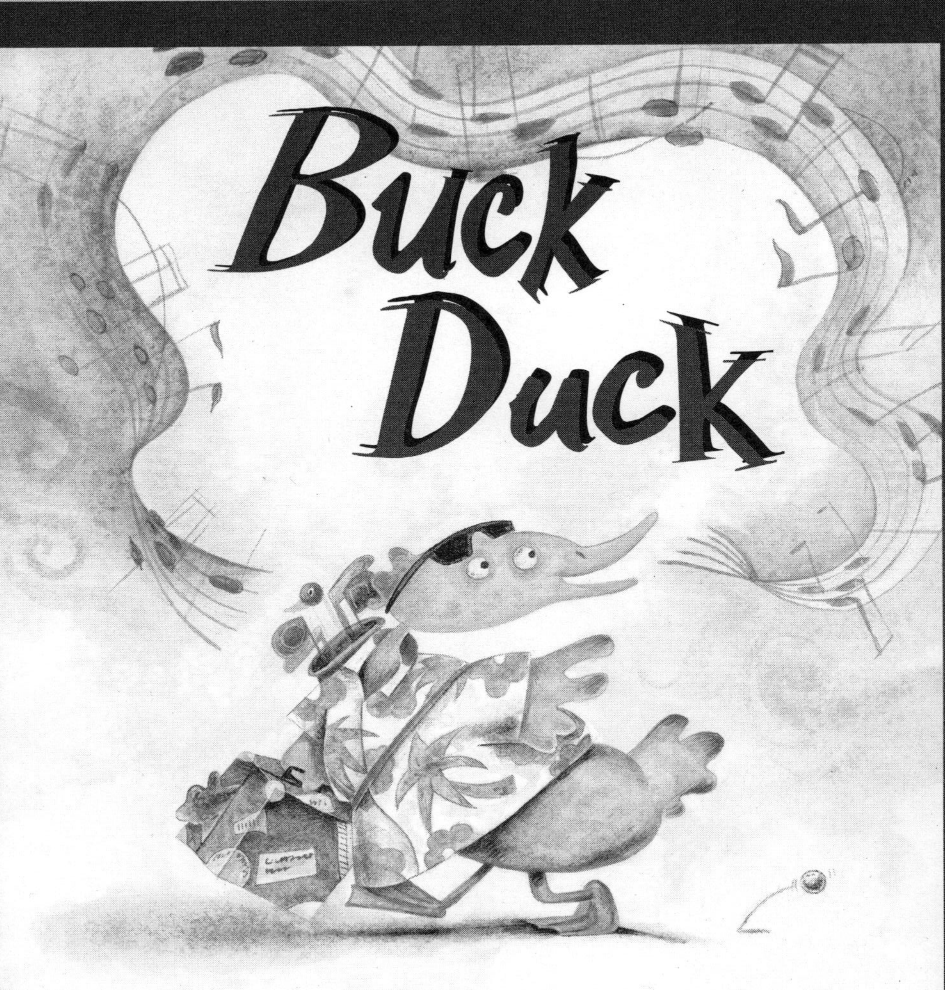

by Gail Williams
illustrated by Marc Mongeau

Buck Duck packed up his truck.

Fold

Fold

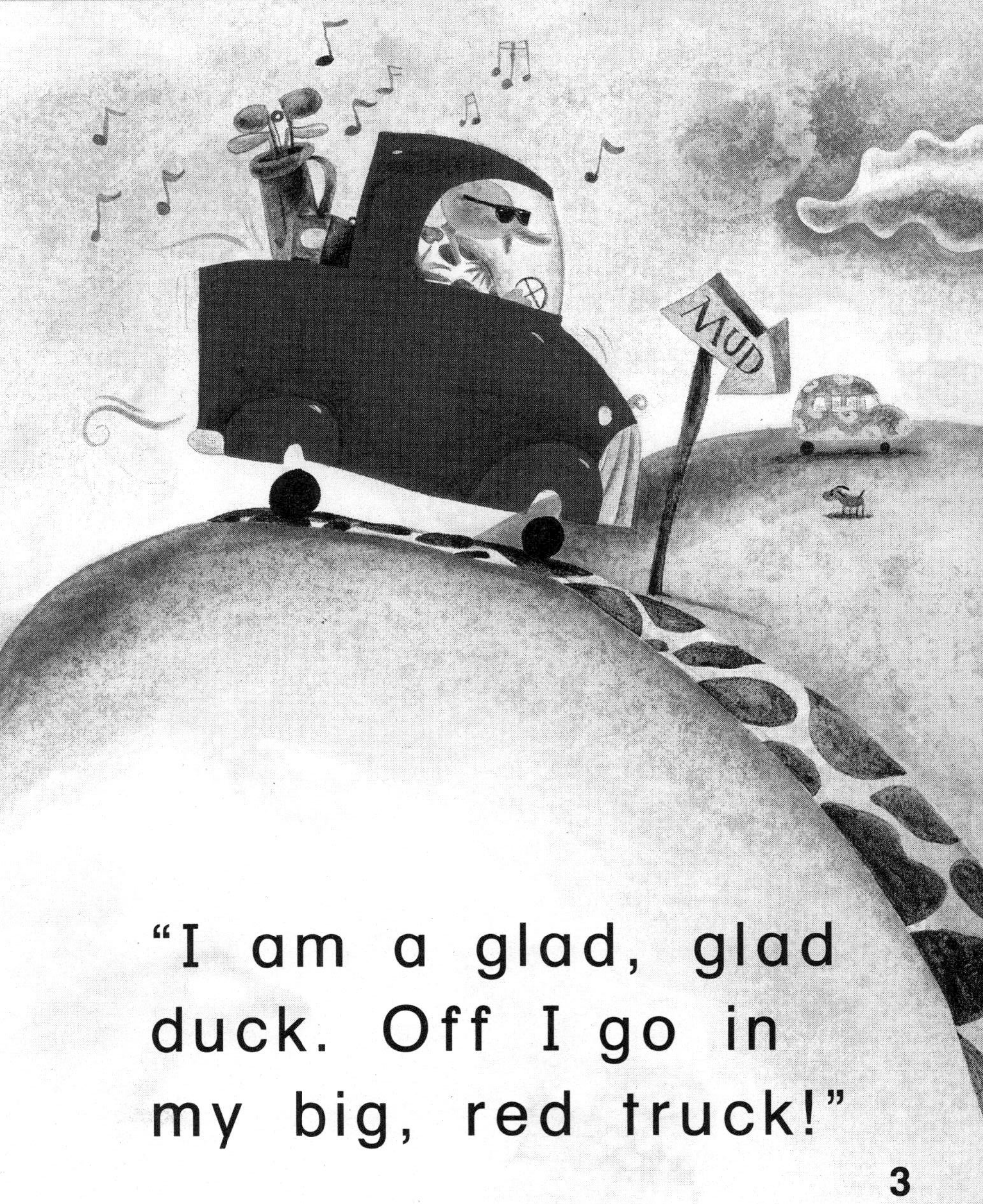

"I am a glad, glad duck. Off I go in my big, red truck!"

"I am NOT a glad, glad duck! Look at this mud. I am stuck!"

Fold

Buck Duck

Word Count: 88

High-Frequency Words

go
my
look
come
me
the
you

Decodable Words*

a	glad	led	**pup's**
am	had	lot	red
at	help	mom	**stuck**
big	his	**mud**	thanks
Buck	**huff**	not	this
bump	I	off	**thump**
bus	if	packed	**truck**
can	in	path	**tug**
Duck	it's	pink	**up**
fun	**jumped**	**puff**	with
get	**just**	**pup**	

*Words with /u/*u* appear in **boldface** type.

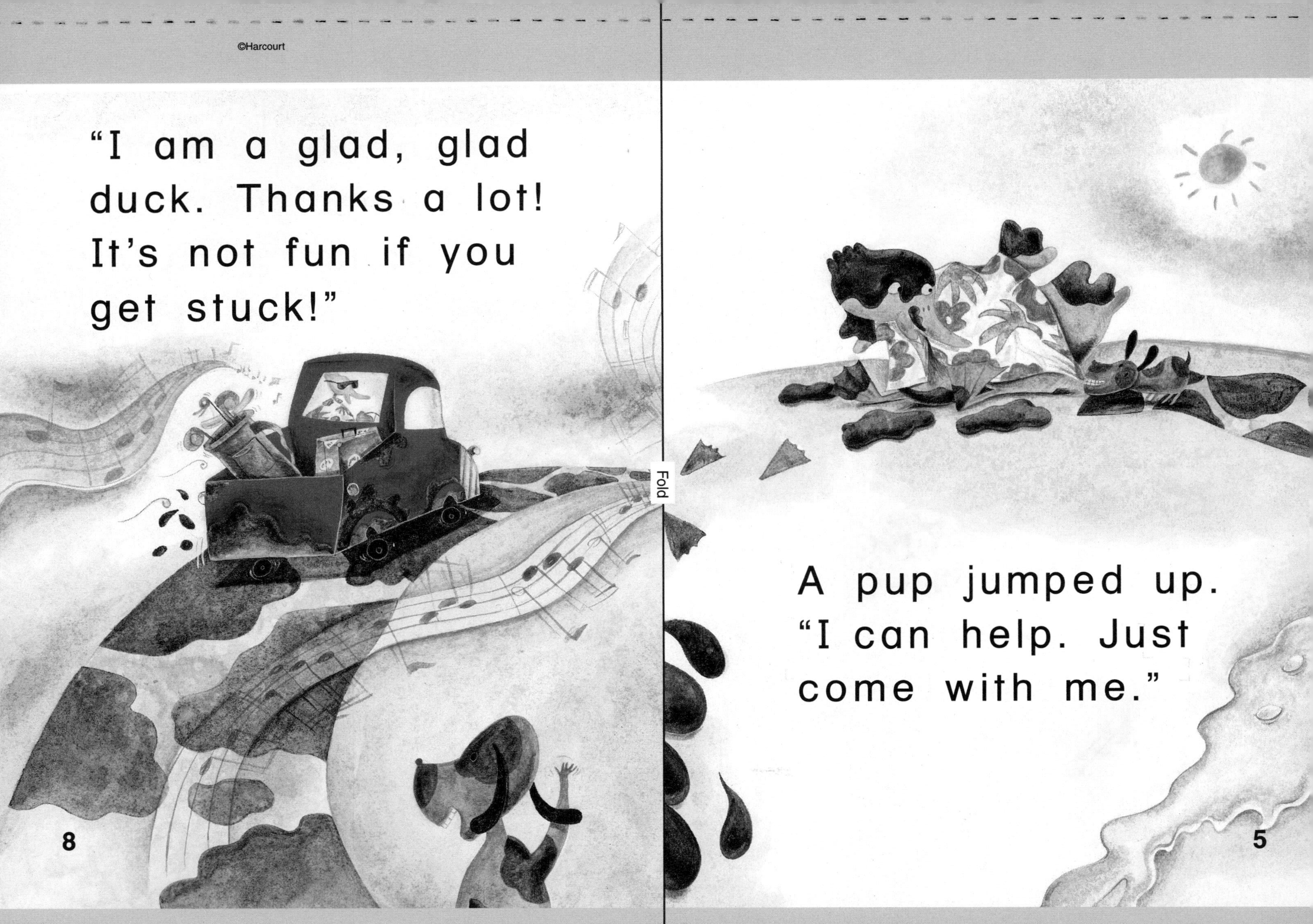

“I am a glad, glad duck. Thanks a lot! It’s not fun if you get stuck!”

Fold

A pup jumped up. “I can help. Just come with me.”

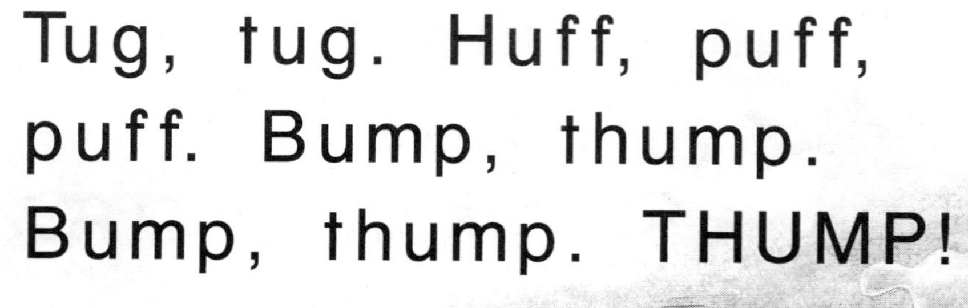

The pup led Buck up a path. The pup's mom had a big, pink bus.

Fold

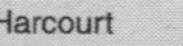

Tug, tug. Huff, puff, puff. Bump, thump. Bump, thump. THUMP!

DECODABLE BOOK 10

King Bing Plays Ball

Fold

King Bing Plays Ball

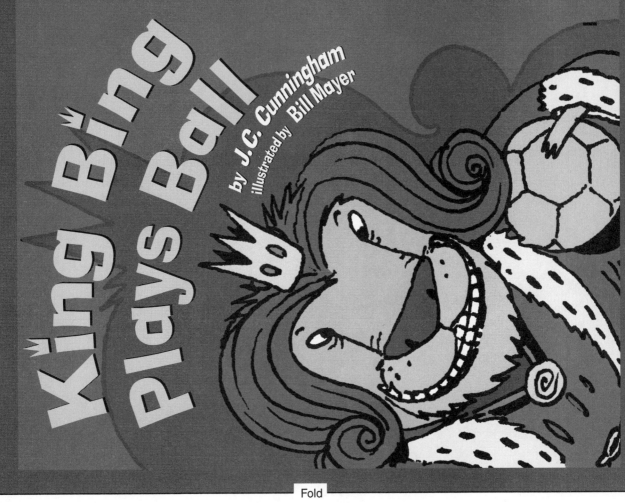

by J.C. Cunningham

illustrated by Bill Mayer

This is King Bing.

Fold

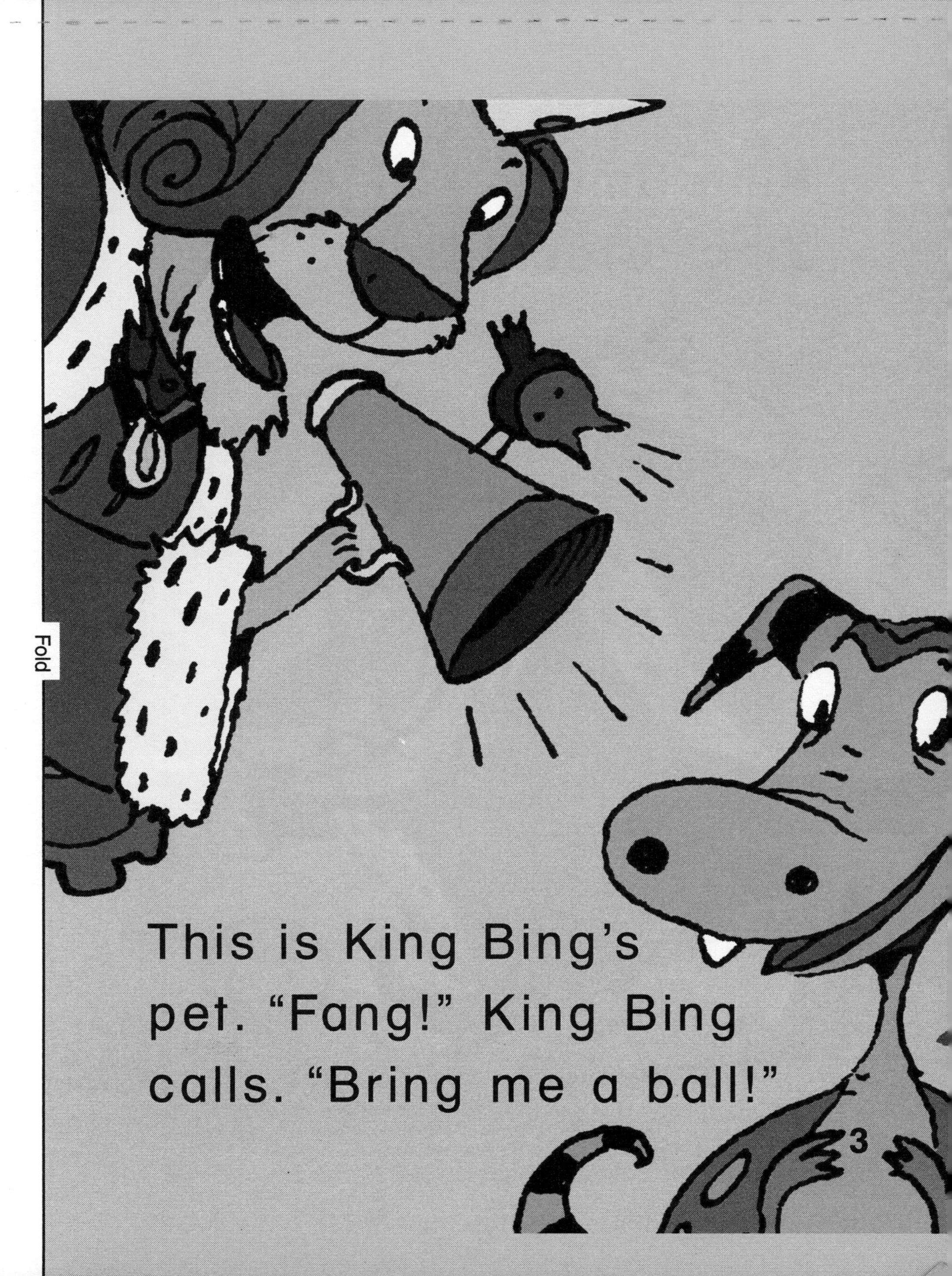

This is King Bing's pet. "Fang!" King Bing calls. "Bring me a ball!"

Fold

King Bing is kicking.
Zing! Crack! Bang!

Fold

King Bing Plays Ball

Word Count: 68

High-Frequency Words

me
plays
the
what
where

Decodable Words*

a	has	**ping**
and	in	**pong**
ball	is	sits
bang	it	spins
Bing	kick	**swings**
Bing's	**kicking**	that
bong	**King**	**thing**
bring	land	thinks
calls	lands	this
crack	**long**	will
Fang	lost	wins
grass	pet	**zing**

*Words with /ng/*ng* appear in **boldface** type.

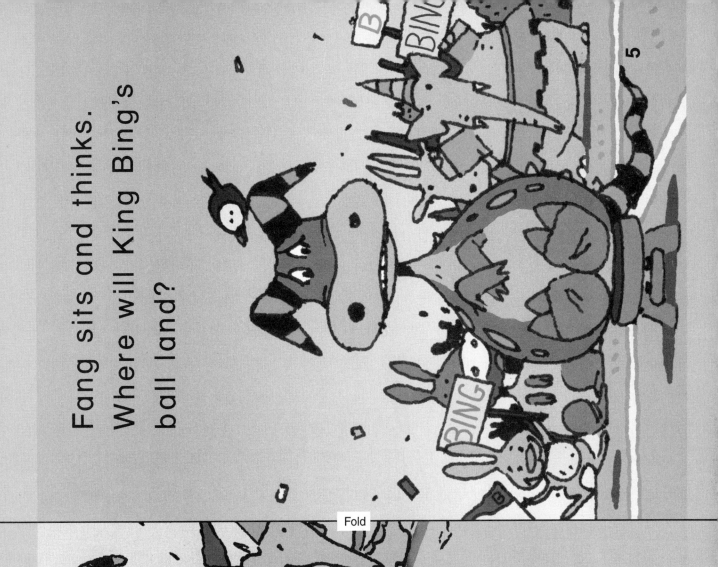

Fang has it! Fang wins!

Fang sits and thinks.
Where will King Bing's
ball land?

What a long kick!
King Bing swings
and spins and lands
in the grass!
Ping! Pong! Bong!

Where is the ball?
Is that thing lost?

DECODABLE BOOK 10
Ling and Lang

Fold

Ling and Lang

by Gail Williams
illustrated by Viv Eisner Hess

Sniff, sniff! Yum, yum!
"A snack!" sings Ling.
"A snack!" sings Lang.

Fold

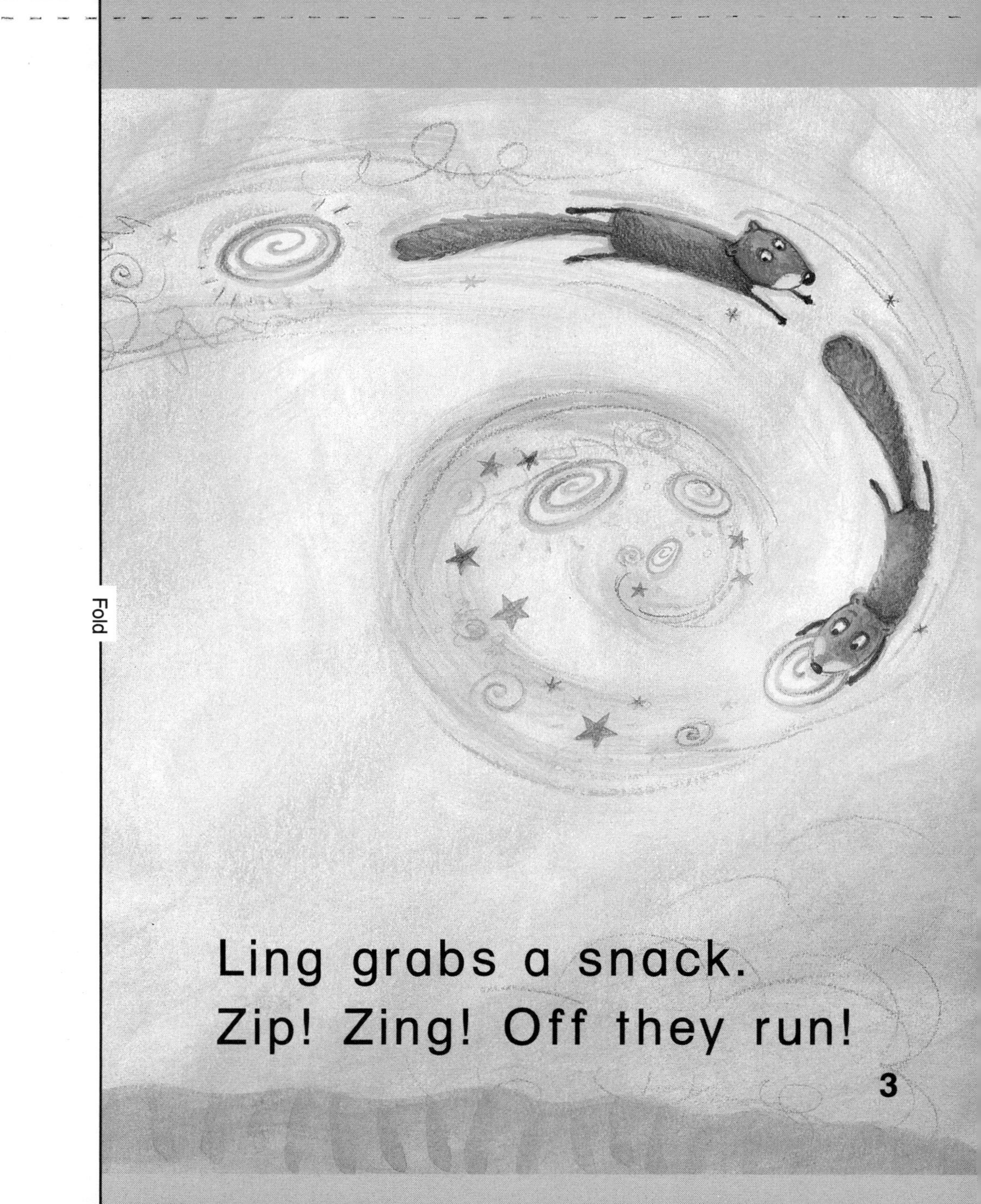

Ling grabs a snack.
Zip! Zing! Off they run!

Fold

Ling swings on a fan.
Lang spins in a pan.

Fold

Ling and Lang

Word Count: 84

High-Frequency Words

are
like
me
of
out
the
they
too
where

Decodable Words*

a	**Lang**	snacks
all	**Ling**	sniff
and	Mom	spins
bring	moms	**swings**
calls	off	**thinking**
falls	on	yum
fan	pan	**zing**
grabs	run	zip
in	**sings**	
is	snack	

*Words with /ng/*ng* appear in **boldface** type.

"Ling! Lang!" Mom calls.
"Bring me a snack!
Moms like snacks, too!"

Fold

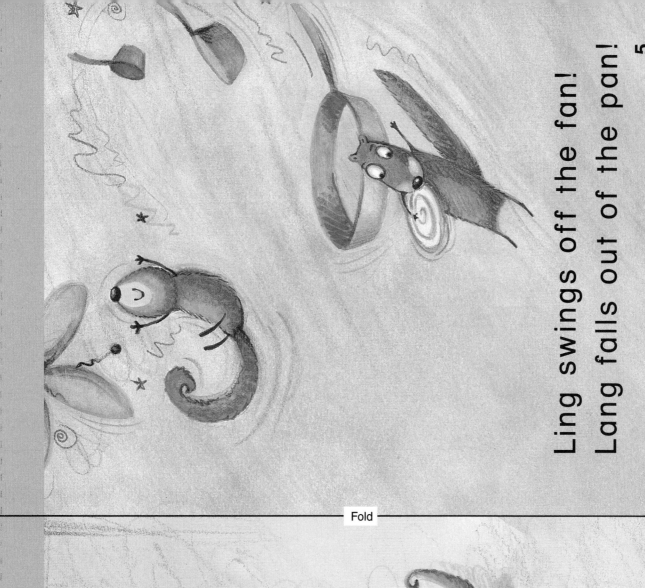

Ling swings off the fan!
Lang falls out of the pan!

Ling is thinking,
"Where is Lang?"
Lang is thinking,
"Where is Ling?"

Fold

Mom is thinking, too!
"Where is Ling?
Where is Lang? Where
are all the snacks?"

DECODABLE BOOK 11
Morning Song

Fold

Morning Song

by Mary Hogan • illustrated by Nancy Davis

Fold

In the morning, Doris
runs in the sun.

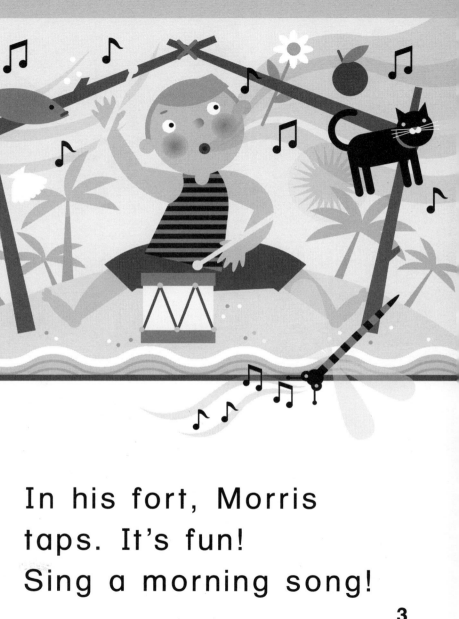

In his fort, Morris
taps. It’s fun!
Sing a morning song!

Gram hums and rocks
back and forth.

Fold

Morning Song

Word Count: 70

High-Frequency Words

someone
the
too
you

Decodable Words*

a	his	rocks
and	hops	runs
Ann	hums	singing
back	in	sings
corn	is	skips
Doris	it	song
flips	it's	spins
flops	**morning**	**storm**
fort	**Morris**	sun
forth	Nan	tall
fun	**Norm**	taps
Gram	**North**	

*Words with /ôr/*or* appear in **boldface** type.

Someone is singing.
Is it you?
Sing! Sing a morning
song, too!

Fold

Nan sings and spins in
the North.
Sing a morning song!

In the tall corn,
Norm flips and flops.

In a storm,
Ann skips and hops.
Sing a morning song!

DECODABLE BOOK 11
Mort's Trip to the Store

Fold

Mort's Trip to the Store

by Stephanie Saal
illustrated by Sarah Beise

Dad sent Mort to
the store. “Stop, Mort!
Don’t forget this!”

Fold

Fold

Mort wore his best cap.
Mort didn't forget that!

Mort went off,
but he had to stop
and play ball.

Fold

Mort's Trip to the Store

Word Count: 89

High-Frequency Words

don't
he
new
play
the
to
what
you

Decodable Words*

a	didn't	Mort's	that
and	felt	off	this
asked	for	ran	**tore**
at	forget	rest	trip
ball	get	**score**	up
best	got	sent	went
but	had	**snore**	**wore**
cap	his	**sore**	
Dad	last	stop	
did	Mort	**store**	

*Words with /ôr/*ore* appear in **boldface** type.

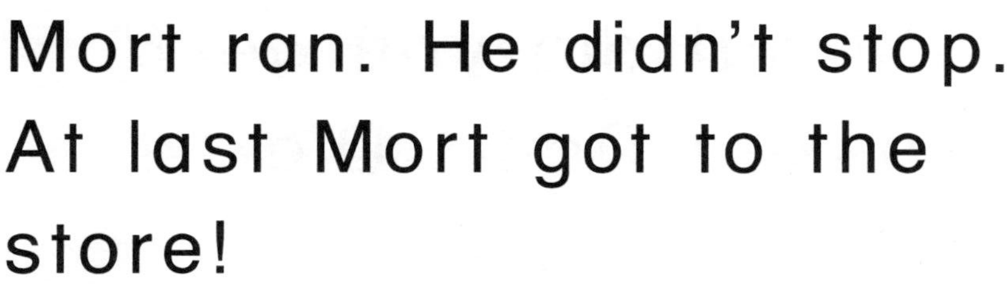

Mort ran. He didn't stop. At last Mort got to the store!

Fold

Mort got a score, but he felt sore. Mort had to stop and rest. Snore, snore, snore.

Mort got up, but his cap tore. He had to stop for a new cap.

Fold

"What did you get?" asked Dad. "Did you forget?"

DECODABLE BOOK 11
The Fort

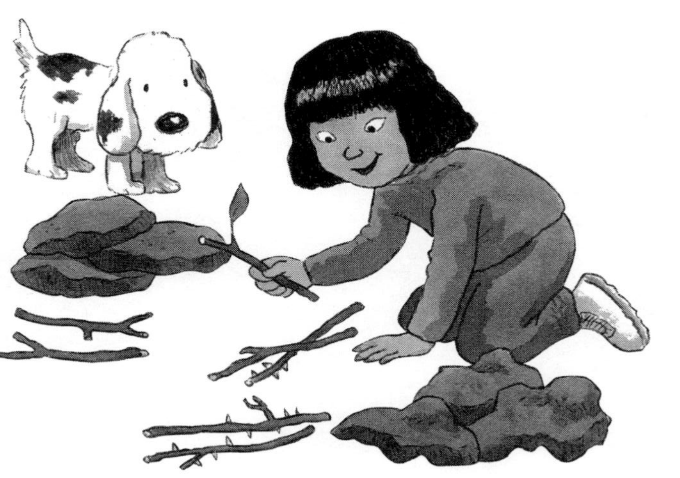

Fold

The Fort

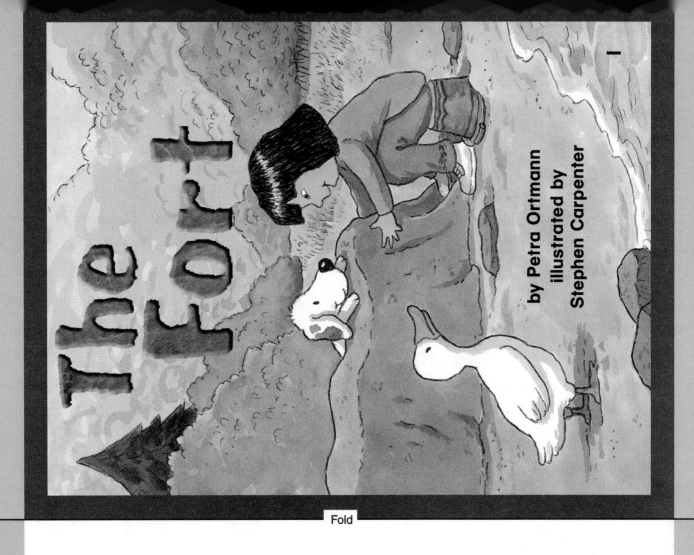

by Petra Ortmann
illustrated by
Stephen Carpenter

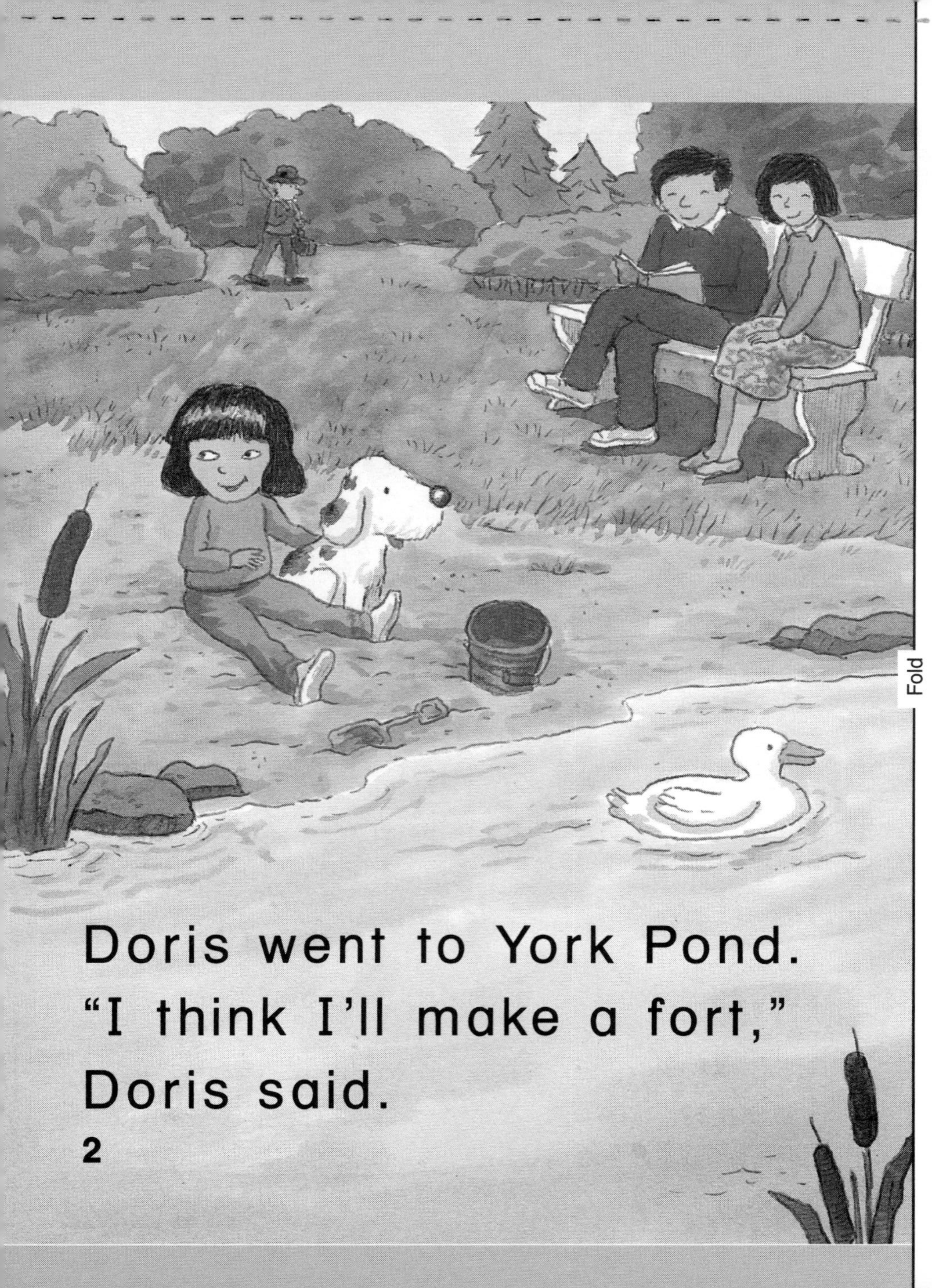

Doris went to York Pond.
"I think I'll make a fort,"
Doris said.

Fold

Fold

Doris dug in the sand.
She formed a big wall.

Then Doris sorted twigs and rocks. "No twigs with thorns," said Doris. "No rocks with bumps."

Fold

The Fort

Word Count: 87

High-Frequency Words

make
new
night
no
oh
said
she
the
to
was

Decodable Words*

a	grand	sand	well
and	I	**sorted**	went
back	I'll	**stormed**	wet
big	in	sunk	wind
bumps	it	that	with
Doris	it's	then	**York**
dug	**morning**	think	
formed	next	**thorns**	
fort	**north**	tossed	
forth	pond	twigs	
fun	rocks	wall	

*Words with /ôr/*or* appear in **boldface** type.

"Oh, well," said Doris.
"I'll make a new fort.
I think it's fun!"

The fort was grand!

That night, it stormed. The north wind tossed the twigs back and forth. The rocks sunk in the wet sand.

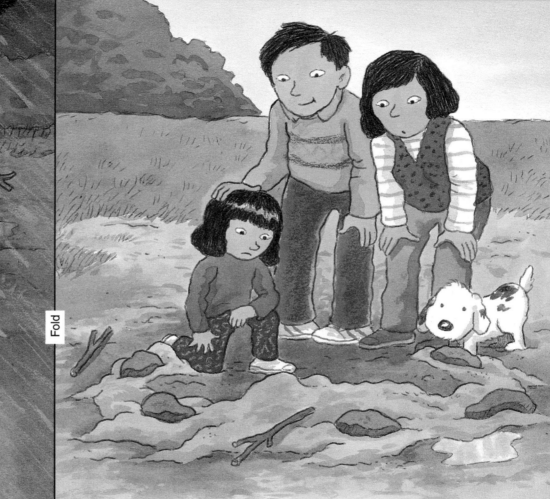

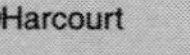

Fold

The next morning, Doris went back to York Pond.

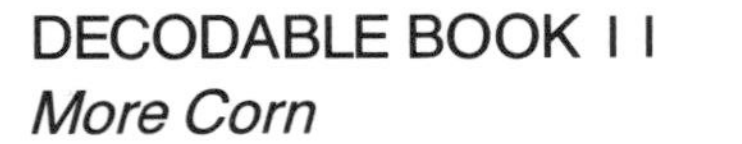
DECODABLE BOOK 11
More Corn

Fold

More Corn

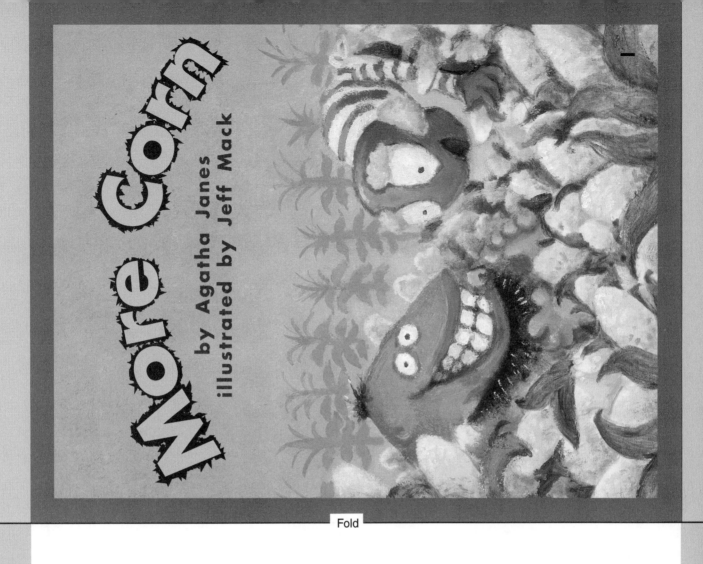

by Agatha Janes
illustrated by Jeff Mack

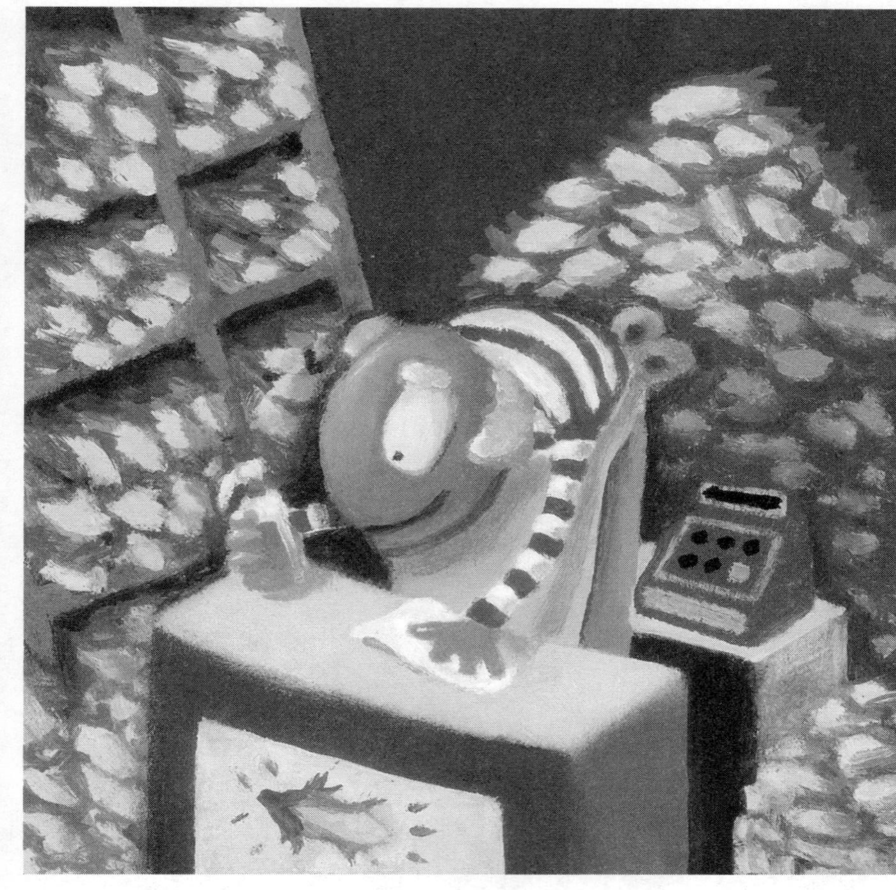

Corwin had a store. He had lots of corn to sell.

Fold

Corwin put up a big ad.

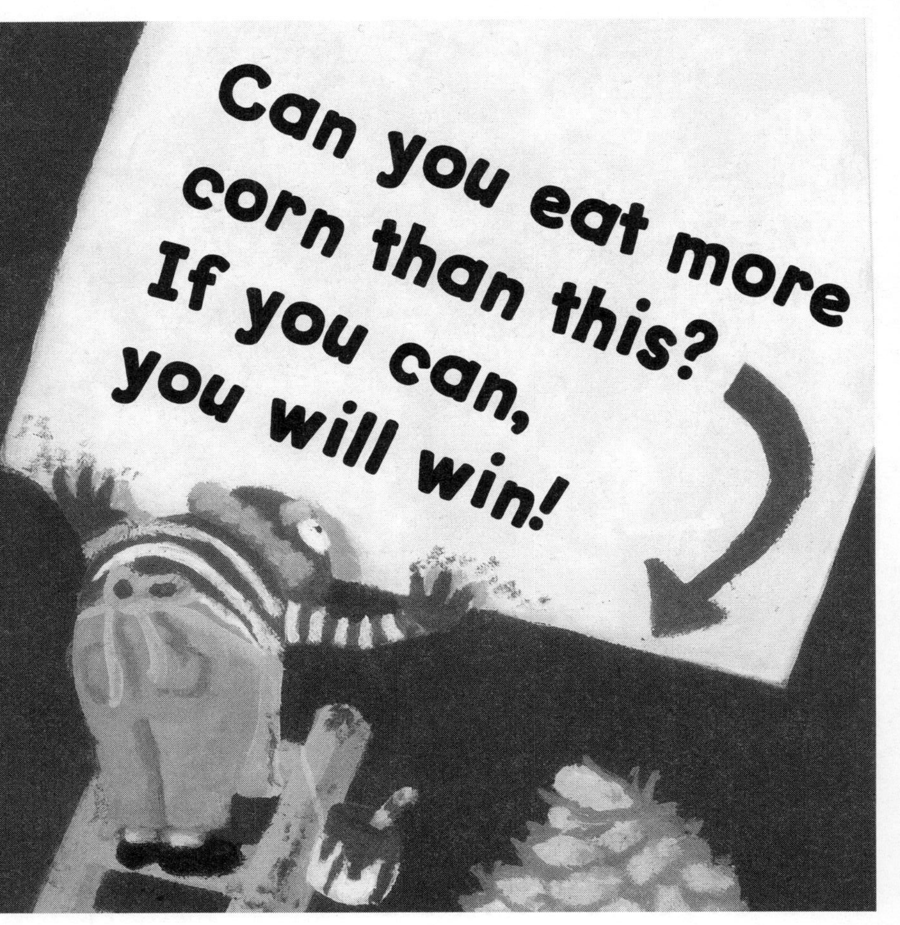
Can you eat more
corn than this?
If you can,
you will win!

Fold

Boris went to Corwin's store. "I can win," Boris snorted.

Fold

More Corn

Word Count: 88

High-Frequency Words

are
eat
eating
he
my
of
put
to
what
you

Decodable Words*

a	Corwin	**more**	**tore**
ad	Corwin's	**score**	up
all	did	sell	went
and	had	snorted	will
bib	his	**sore**	win
big	I	stop	**wore**
Boris	if	**store**	yelled
called	kept	than	
can	lips	then	
corn	lots	this	

*Words with /ôr/*ore* appear in **boldface** type.

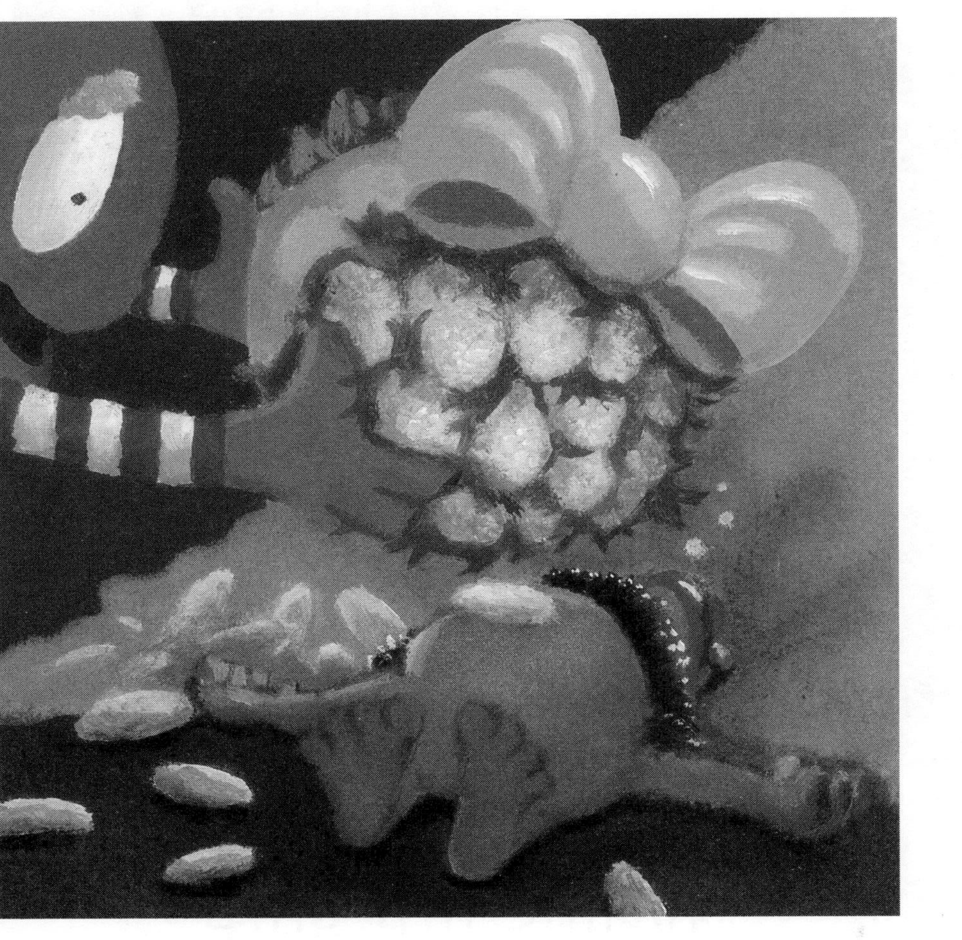

"More corn!"

Fold

Boris wore a big bib. Corwin kept score, and Boris kept eating. "More corn!" Boris called.

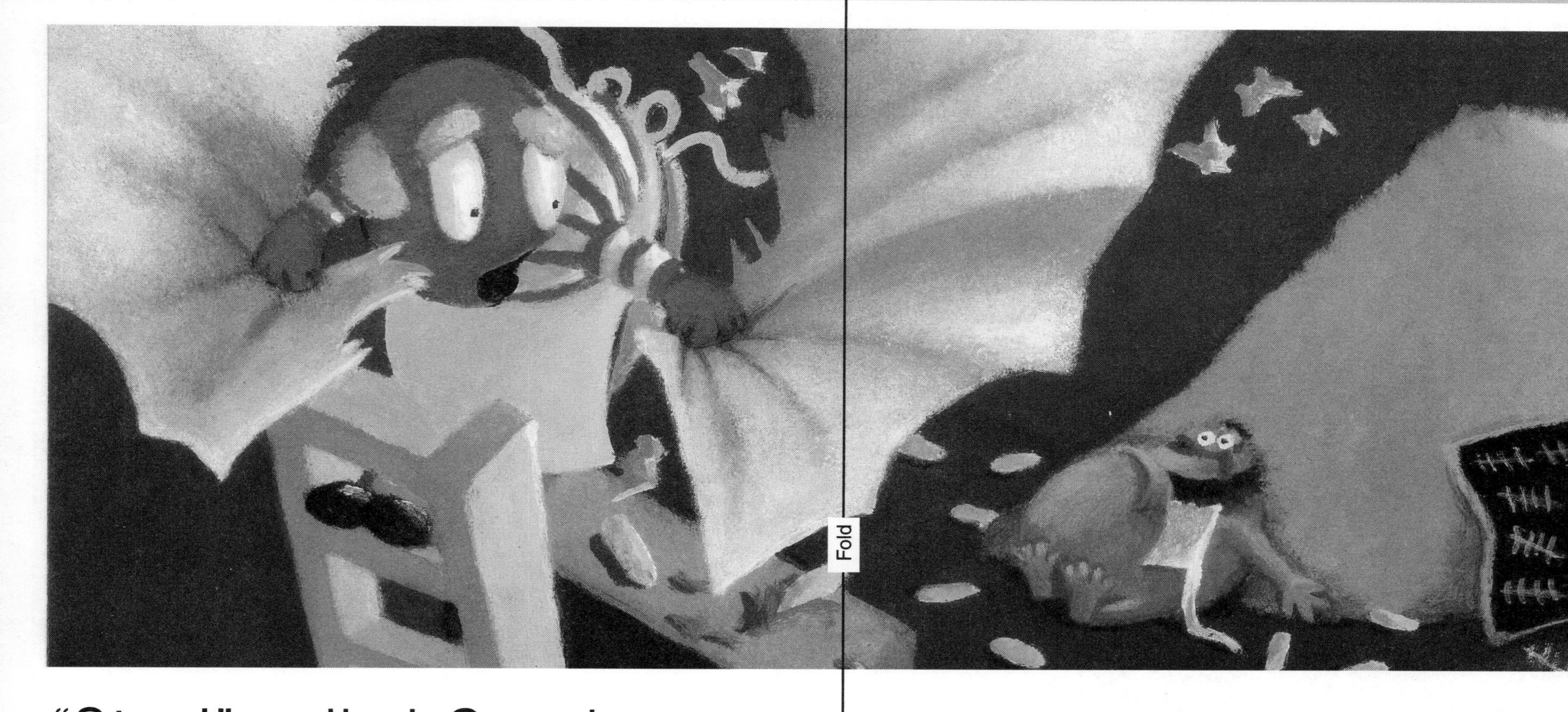

"Stop!" yelled Corwin.
"You are eating up all
my corn! You win!" Then
Corwin tore up his ad.

"My lips are sore,"
snorted Boris.
"What did I win?"

DECODABLE BOOK 12
At the Shore

Fold

At the Shore

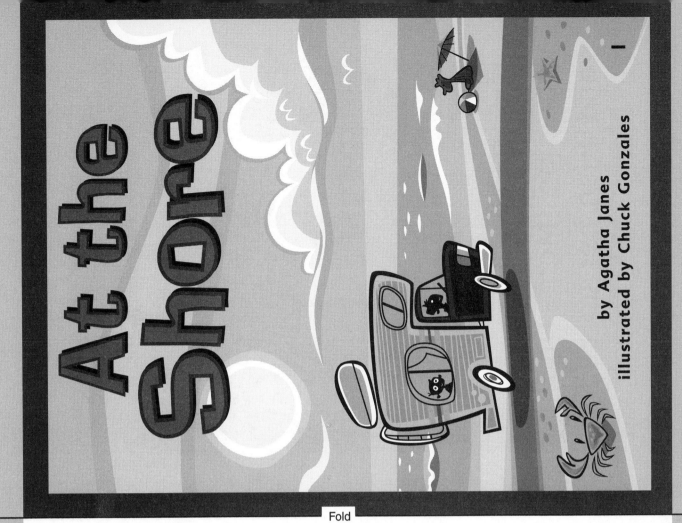

by Agatha Janes
illustrated by Chuck Gonzales

The Smiths went camping. Mom, Dad, and Trish set up camp.

Fold

Fold

Josh dashed off, but Mom called him back. “Don’t rush off without us!”

"Gosh," grunted Josh.
"This isn't fun."
"Hush," Trish said.
"You'll have fun."

Fold

At the Shore

Word Count: 88

High-Frequency Words

could	put	you'll
don't	said	
go	saw	
have	the	
he	we	
of	without	

Decodable Words*

a	**fishing**	**Josh**	**shore**
and	fun	lots	Smiths
at	**gosh**	man	swam
back	got	Mom	that
big	grunted	off	then
but	had	on	this
called	helped	picked	**Trish**
camp	him	rods	up
camping	his	**rush**	us
Dad	**hush**	set	went
dashed	I	**shed**	**wish**
did	in	**shells**	
fish	isn't	**ship**	

*Words with /sh/*sh* appear in **boldface** type.

Josh got his wish!

Fold

Josh <u>did</u> have fun. He swam and saw lots of fish. He picked up shells.

Josh helped a man put
fishing rods in a shed.
Then Josh saw a big ship.

Fold

"I had fun," said Josh,
"but I wish we could
go on that ship."

DECODABLE BOOK 12
Trash

Fold

Trash

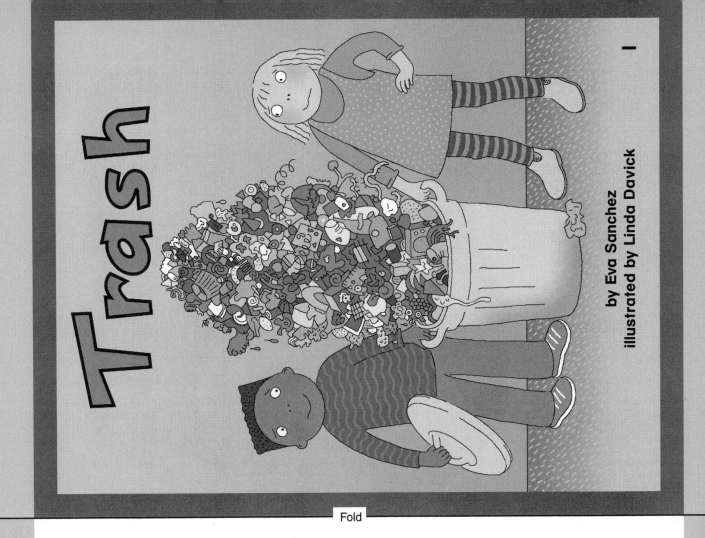

by Eva Sanchez
illustrated by Linda Davick

Big stores have trash.
Small shops have trash.

Fold

Fold

We all have trash!
We toss it into short
bins and tall bins.
What happens to it?

Bam! Bang! Crash!
Big trucks pick up trash.
They mash it, crush it,
and smash it.

Fold

Trash

Word Count: 88

High-Frequency Words

do	they
don't	to
have	use
into	we
make	what
new	

Decodable Words*

a	dumped	**short**
all	fill	small
and	gets	**smash**
at	happens	sort
bam	I	stores
bang	it	tall
big	just	that
bins	land	things
can	let's	toss
crash	**mash**	**trash**
crush	more	trucks
didn't	pick	up
dump	**shops**	**wish**

*Words with /sh/*sh* appear in **boldface** type.

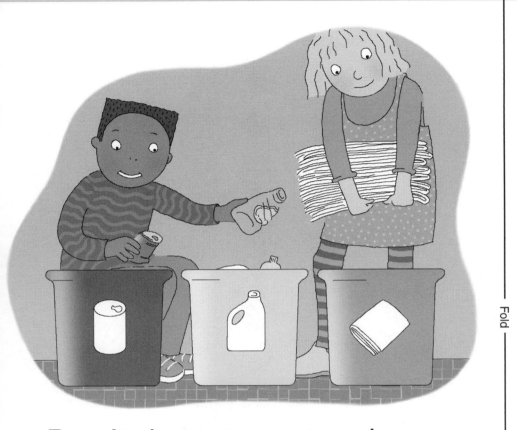

Don't just toss trash into trash bins. Sort it. Let's use trash to make new things!

Fold

It gets dumped at a land fill. More trucks dump more and more trash!

I wish we didn't
have all that trash!
What can we do?

Fold

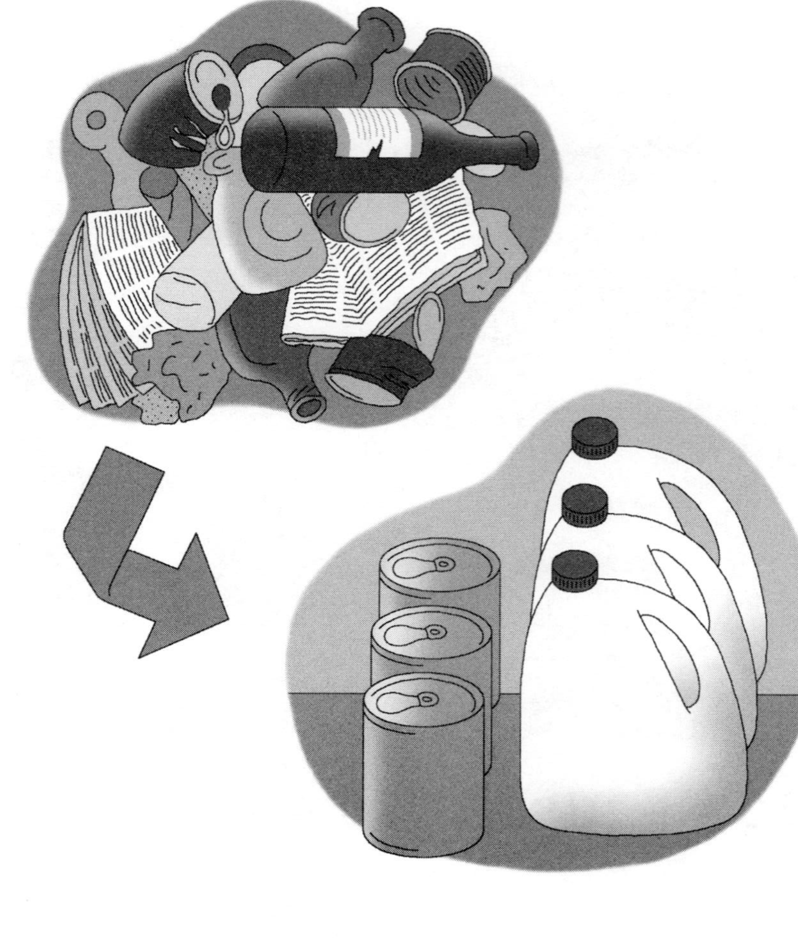

We can <u>use</u> trash!

DECODABLE BOOK 13
Chad and His Chums

Fold

Chad and His Chums

by Waverly Chan
illustrated by Mark A. Hicks

Chad and his chums
went to the mall.
They had so much fun.

Fold

They sat on a bench
and had lunch. Munch,
crunch, crunch.

Fold

Then they went shopping. “Look at this,” Chad called.

Fold

Chad and His Chums

Word Count: 89

High-Frequency Words

look
of
oh
out
said
so
the
they
to
we
what

Decodable Words*

a	**chess**	got	red
all	**chest**	granddad	sat
and	**Chuck**	had	set
at	**Chuck's**	his	shopping
bench	**chums**	lots	stuff
Blanch	**crunch**	**lunch**	then
Blanch's	dad	mall	this
bunch	did	mom	us
called	for	**much**	went
Chad	forgot	mums	
Chad's	fun	**munch**	
check	get	on	

*Words with /ch/*ch* appear in **boldface** type.

"Oh!" they all said.
"We forgot to get
stuff for us!"

Fold

"Check this out," called
Blanch. "Look at this,"
called Chuck.

Chad and his chums got lots of stuff. What did they get?

Fold

A chess set for Chad's dad. A bunch of mums for Blanch's mom. A red chest for Chuck's granddad.

DECODABLE BOOK 13
Mitch and Fitch

Fold

Mitch and Fitch

by Anne Miranda illustrated by David McPhail

Mitch met Fitch at the pond. They wished to catch fish for lunch.

Fold

Fold

Mitch set the latch
on the trap. Fitch sat
on a patch of grass.

Mitch felt a twitch. Fitch felt a pinch and an itch.

Fold

Mitch and Fitch

Word Count: 90

High-Frequency Words

he
of
the
they
to

Decodable Words*

a	flip	met
an	for	**Mitch**
and	got	on
ant	grass	pants
ants	had	**patch**
at	hill	pinch
batch	his	pond
but	in	rid
catch	**itch**	sat
crash	jumped	set
did	landed	trap
felt	**latch**	**twitch**
fish	lost	up
Fitch	lunch	wished

*Words with /ch/*tch* appear in **boldface** type.

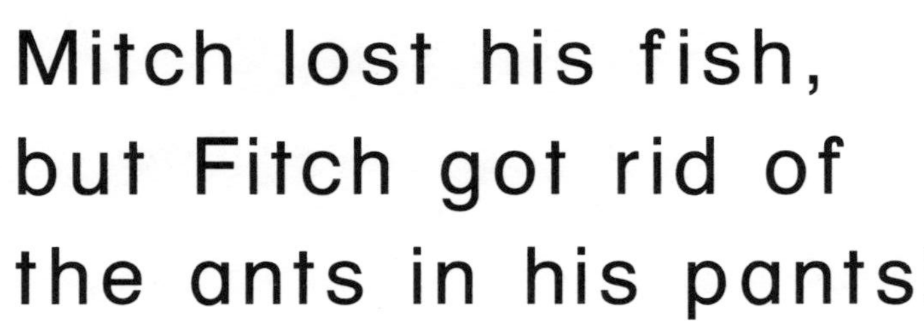

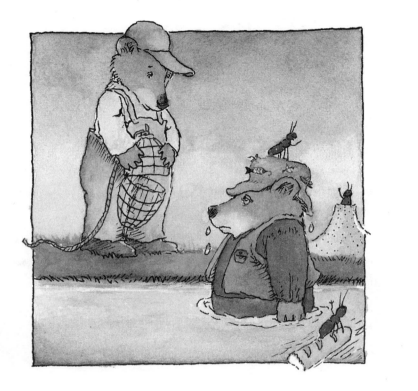

Mitch lost his fish,
but Fitch got rid of
the ants in his pants!

Fold

Mitch got a batch of
fish. Fitch got a batch
of ants in his pants!

Fitch had sat on an ant hill! He jumped up and did a flip.

Fold

Crash! Fitch landed in the pond!

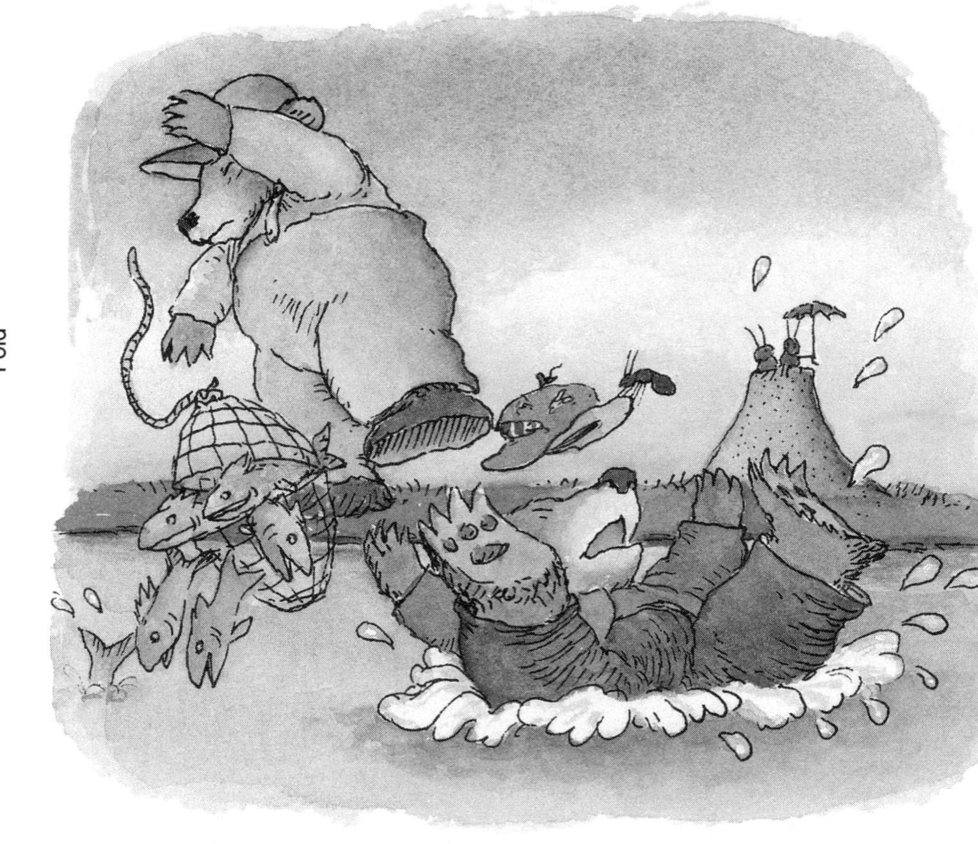

DECODABLE BOOK 13
Chuck and Chet

Fold

Chuck and Chet

by Della Rowland
illustrated by Jackie Urbanovic

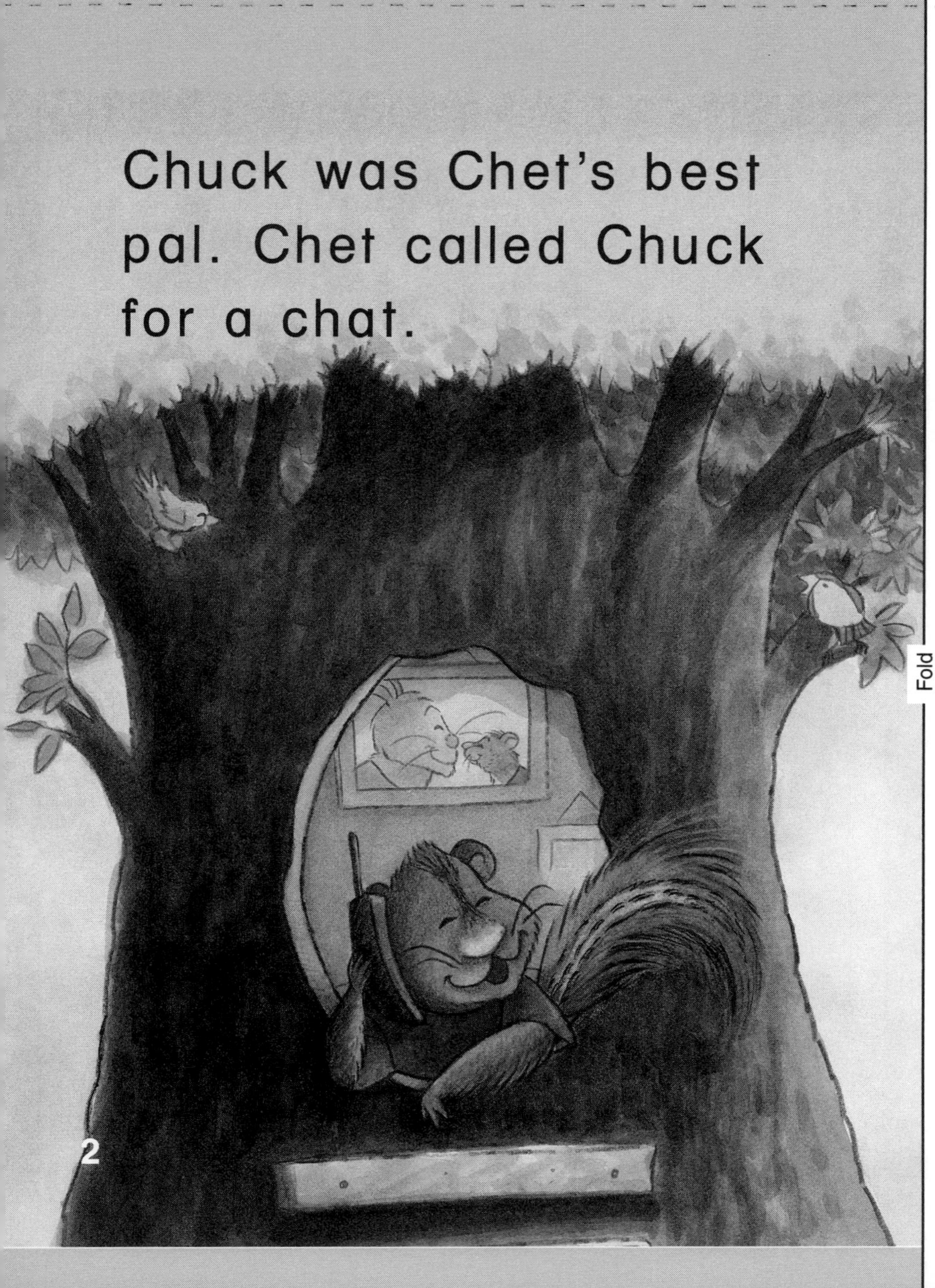

Chuck was Chet's best pal. Chet called Chuck for a chat.

Fold

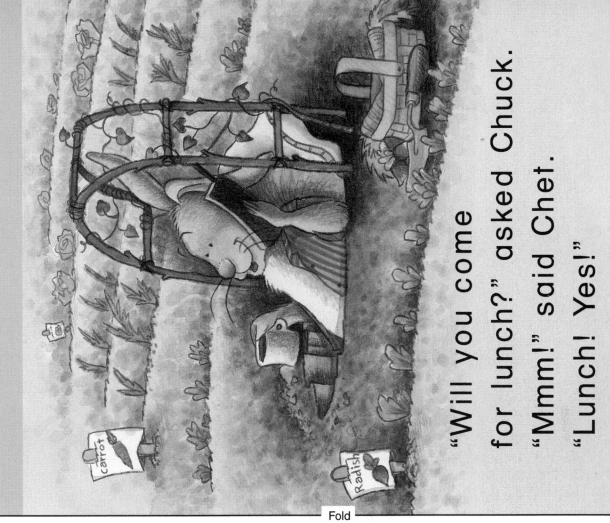

Fold

"Will you come
for lunch?" asked Chuck.
"Mmm!" said Chet.
"Lunch! Yes!"

Chet jumped in his van.
Off he went to Chuck's.
Chug, chug.

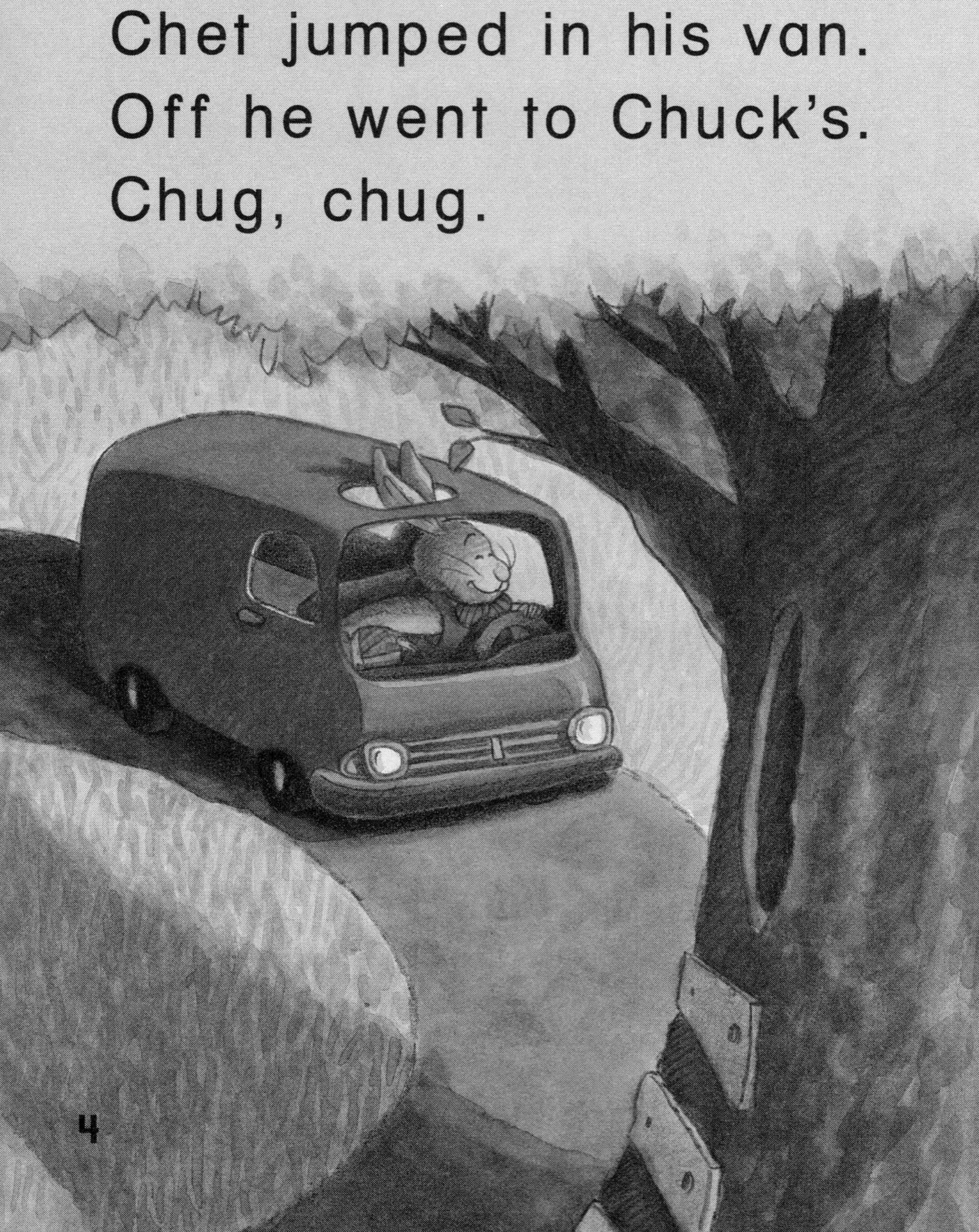

Fold

Chuck and Chet

Word Count: 89

High-Frequency Words

are	of	you
come	said	
have	so	
he	to	
here	too	
looked	was	

Decodable Words*

a	**checked**	I	pal
all	**Chet**	if	pals
am	**Chet's**	in	picnic
and	**Chip**	it	stuff
as	**Chuck**	jumped	van
asked	**Chuck's**	left	went
back	**chug**	**lunch**	will
best	den	mmm	yelled
bunch	for	**much**	yes
called	fun	**munch**	
Chad	had	off	
chat	his	on	

*Words with /ch/*ch* appear in **boldface** type.

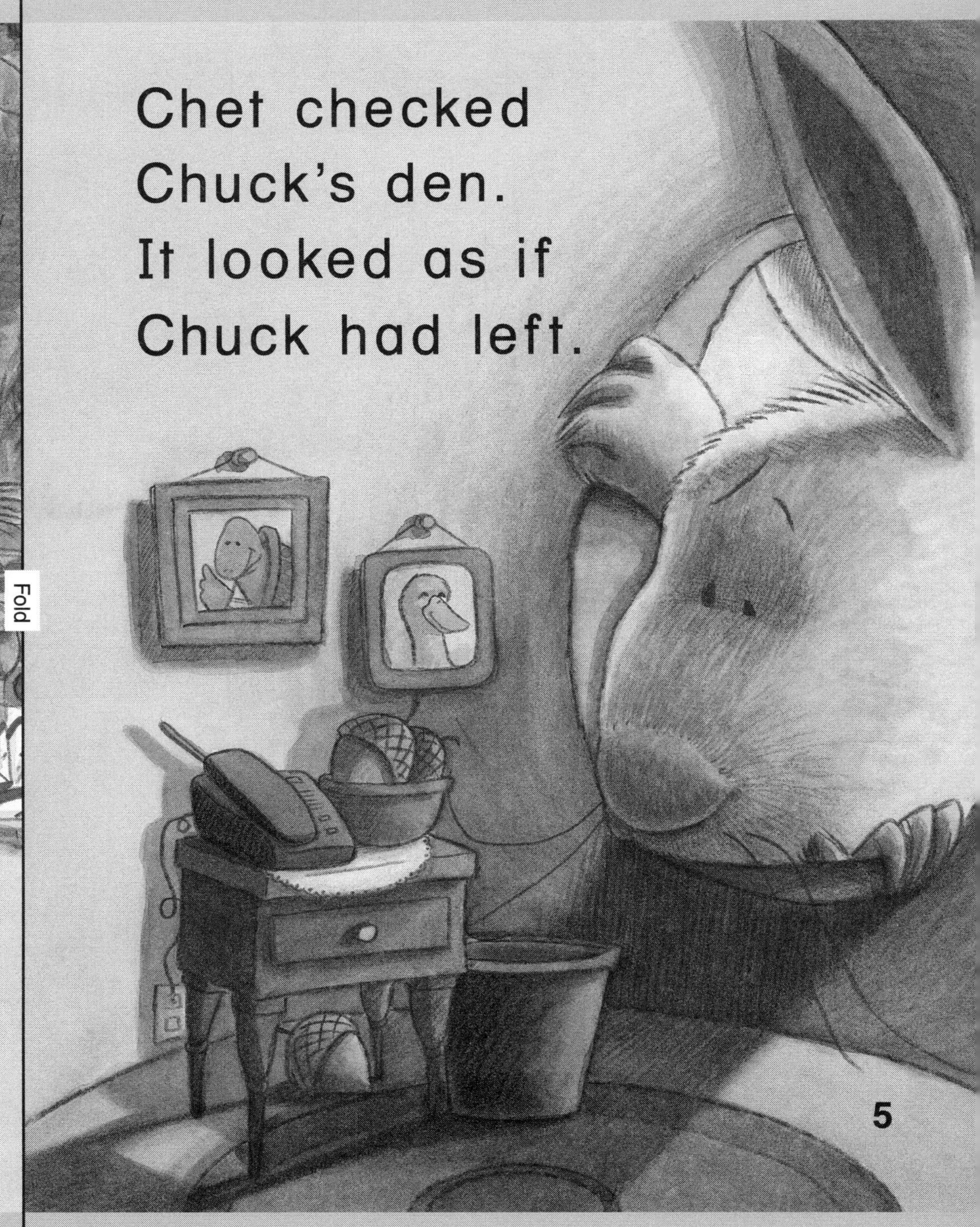

Chet and all his pals
had a picnic lunch.
It was so much fun!

Fold

Chet checked
Chuck's den.
It looked as if
Chuck had left.

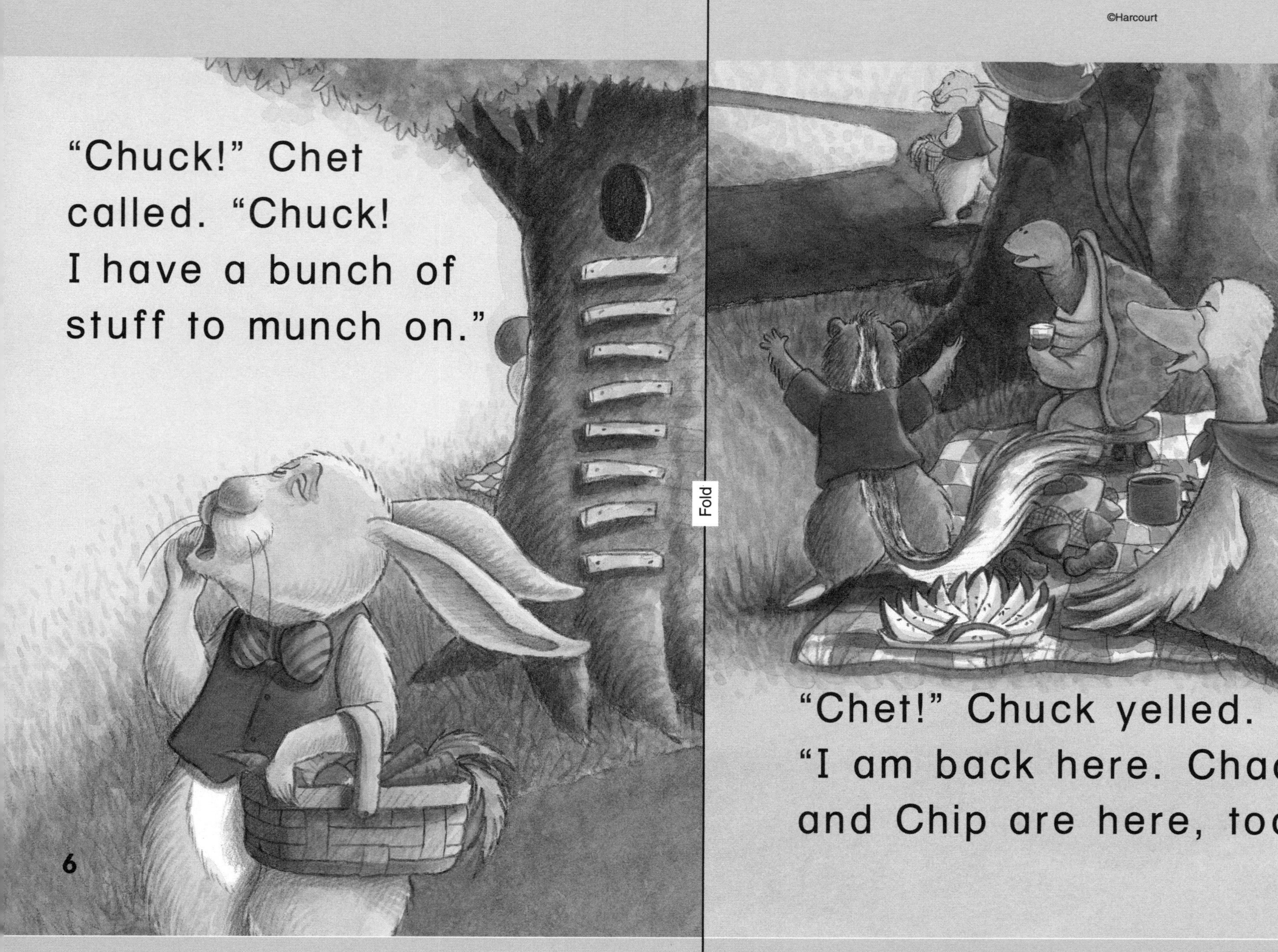

"Chuck!" Chet called. "Chuck! I have a bunch of stuff to munch on."

Fold

"Chet!" Chuck yelled. "I am back here. Chad and Chip are here, too."

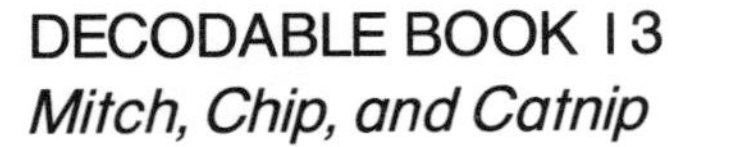

DECODABLE BOOK 13

Mitch, Chip, and Catnip

Fold

Mitch, Chip, and Catnip

by Betsy Franco

illustrated by G.Brian Karas

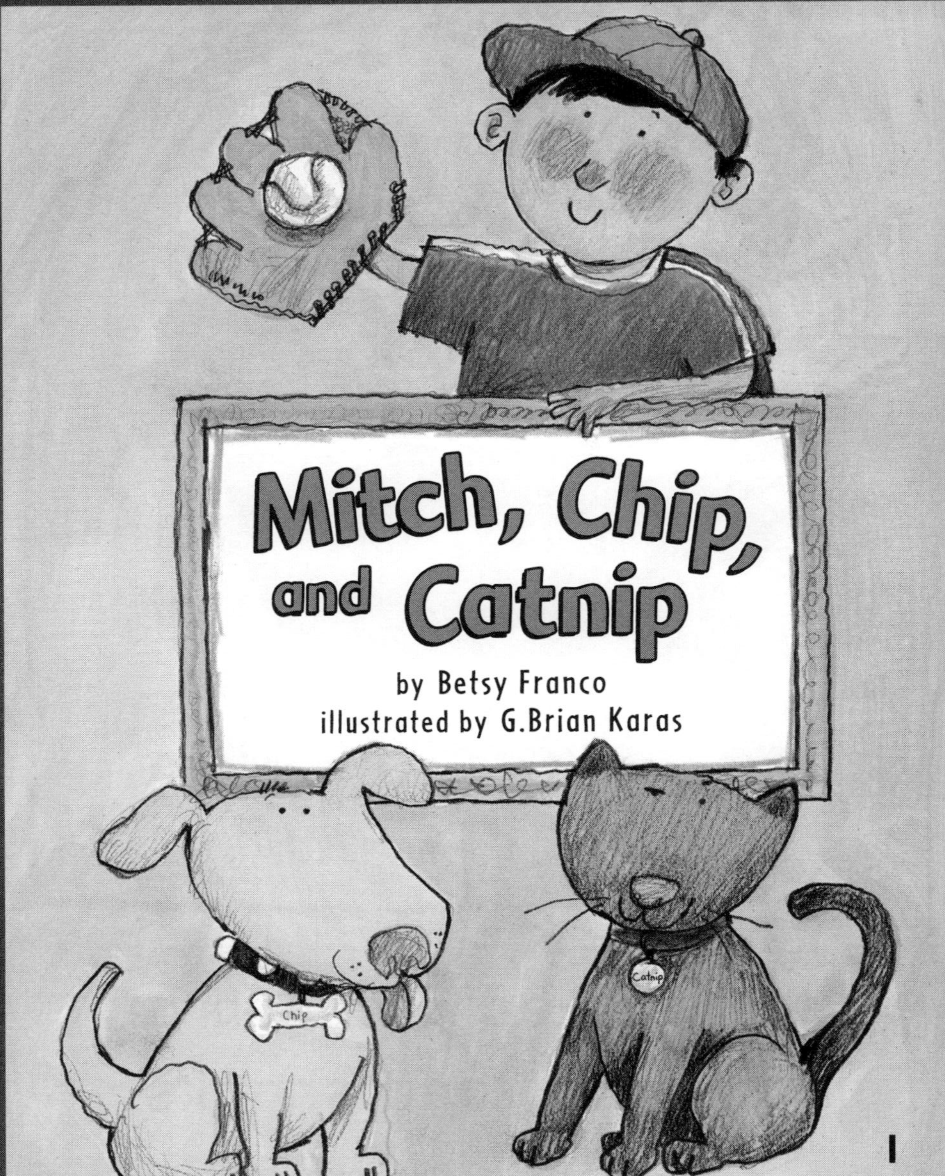

Chip

Catnip

Mitch packed a bunch of mitts, caps, and snacks.

Fold

"Come on, Chip!" called Mitch. "Catnip, you can't come. Cats can't fetch balls."

Fold

Mitch and his pal Fletch went off. Chip went with them.

Fold

Mitch, Chip, and Catnip

Word Count: 80

High-Frequency Words

come
of
she
so
the
they
too
we'll
you

Decodable Words*

a	**catch**	hit	plan
Alex	Catnip	I	snacks
and	cats	I'll	**snatched**
Ann	Chip	**Mitch**	**switch**
balls	**clutched**	mitts	them
bat	**fetch**	much	then
bunch	**Fletch**	off	went
called	fun	on	with
can	had	packed	
can't	**hatched**	pal	
caps	his	**pitch**	

*Words with /ch/*tch* appear in **boldface** type.

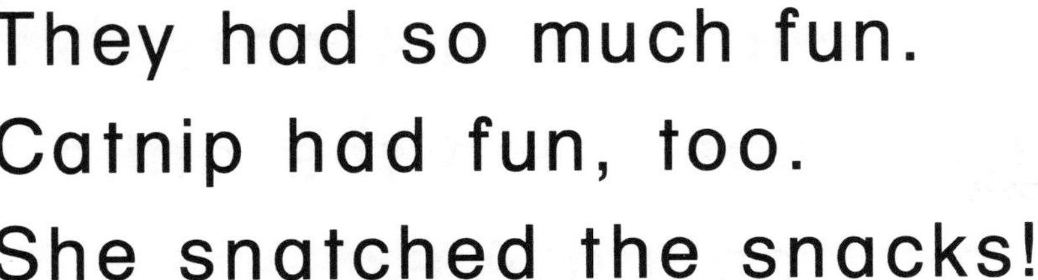

They had so much fun.
Catnip had fun, too.
She snatched the snacks!

Fold

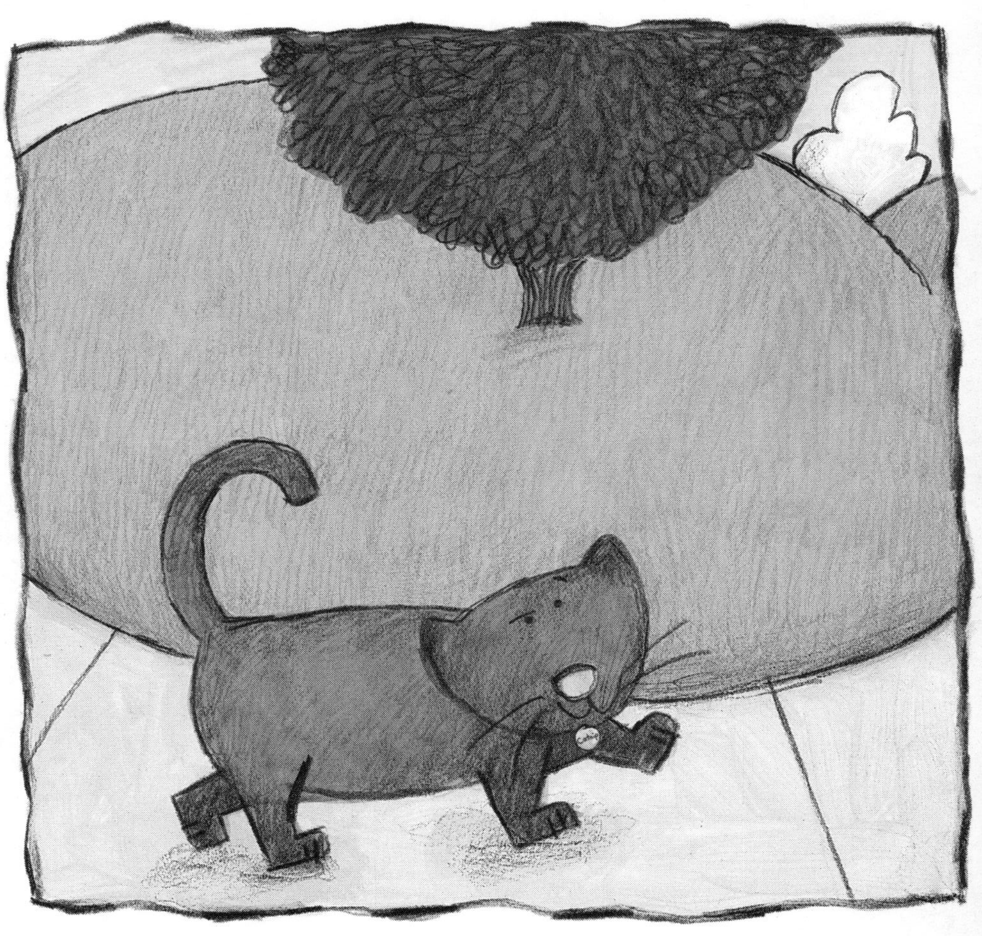

Catnip hatched a plan.
She went, too!

"Mitch!" Ann called.
"I'll catch. You pitch.
Then we'll switch."

Alex clutched his bat.
"Chip can fetch the balls
I hit!" called Alex.

DECODABLE BOOK 14
At the Park

Fold

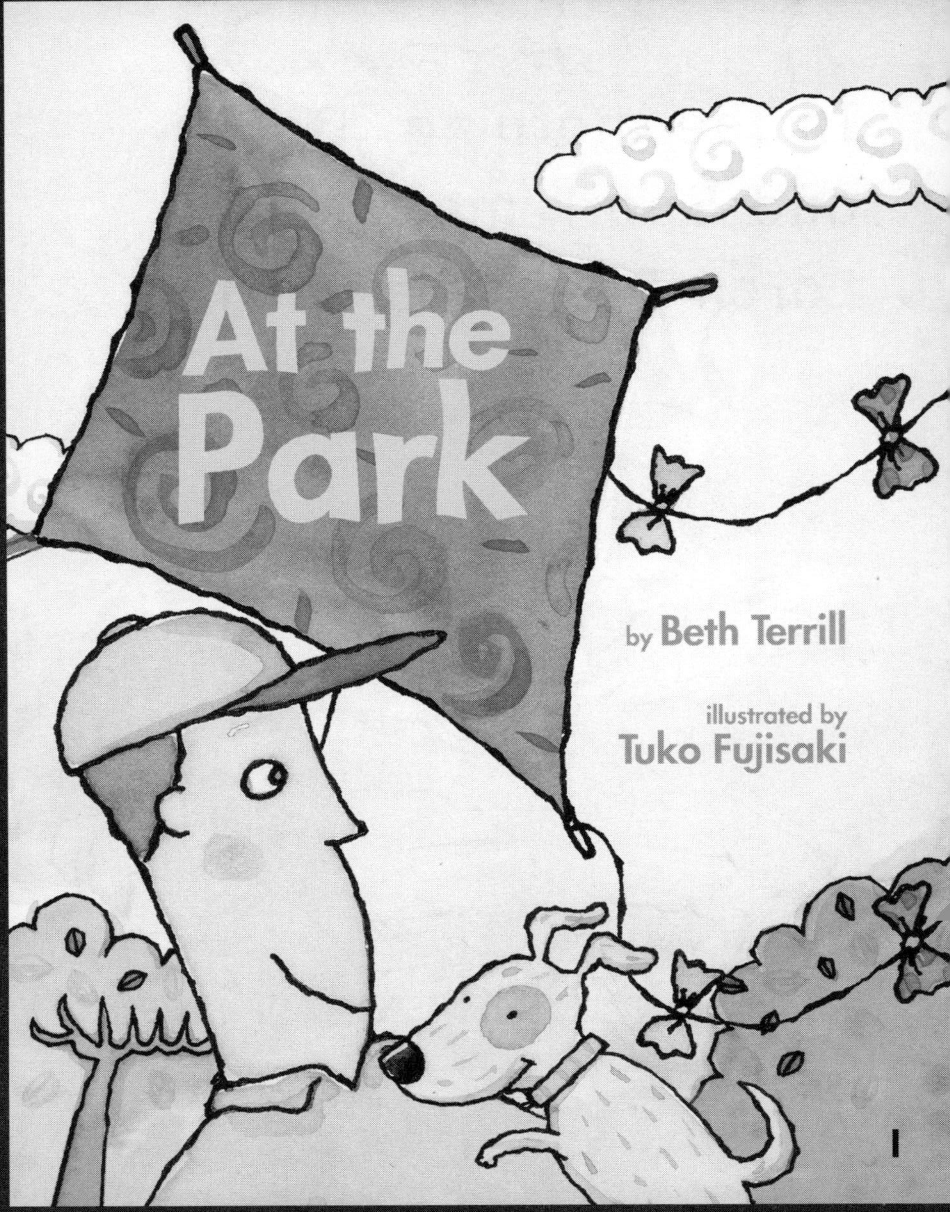

At the Park

by Beth Terrill

illustrated by Tuko Fujisaki

In the morning, Bart and Spark march to Larch Park. It's not far.

Fold

Fold

Bart tugs his little red cart. Spark barks. Arf, arf!

Bart bats a ball. Smack! Spark darts off and catches it! Arf, arf!

Fold

At the Park

Word Count: 99

High-Frequency Words

are	to
he's	too
her	
little	
sees	
she	
so	
the	

Decodable Words*

a	**Clark**	is	red
and	**Clark's**	it	smack
arf	**darts**	it's	**smart**
at	dog	**Larch**	snack
ball	fans	last	**Spark**
barks	**far**	**march**	**start**
Bart	fun	**market**	**starts**
bats	get	Miss	thinks
can't	gets	morning	tugs
car	glad	not	will
cart	his	off	
catches	in	**park**	

*Words with /är/*ar* appear in **boldface** type.

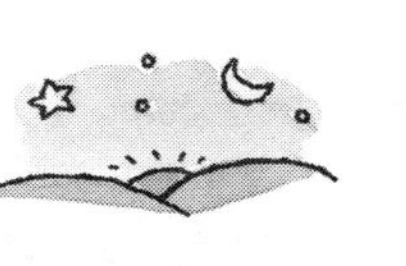

Bart thinks Larch Park is fun. Spark thinks so, too! Arf, arf!

Fold

Bart gets a snack. Spark will get a snack, too. He's a smart dog!

Bart sees Miss Clark. Her car will not start. She can't get to the market. Bart fans the car. Spark barks. Arf, arf!

Fold

At last Miss Clark's car starts! Bart and Spark are glad.

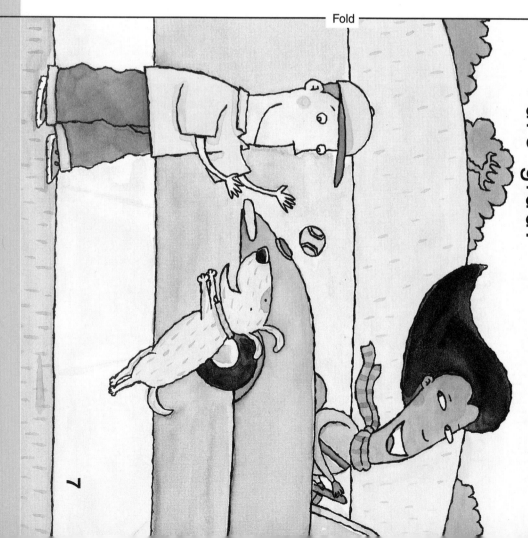

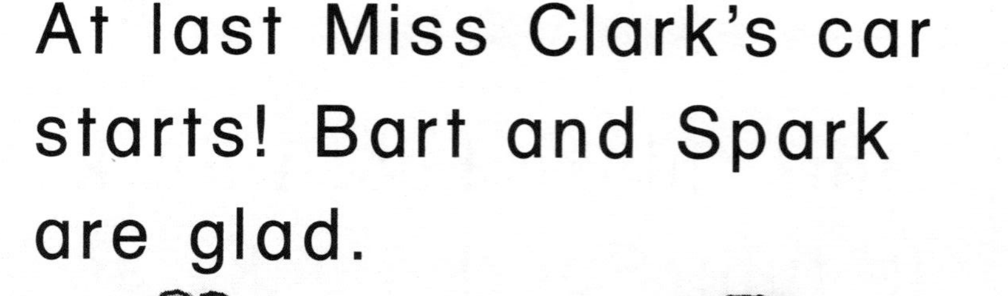

DECODABLE BOOK 14

Back on the Farm

Fold

Back on the Farm

by Eva Sanchez
illustrated by Jill Newton

"I wish I was back on the farm," said Carmen.

Fold

Fold

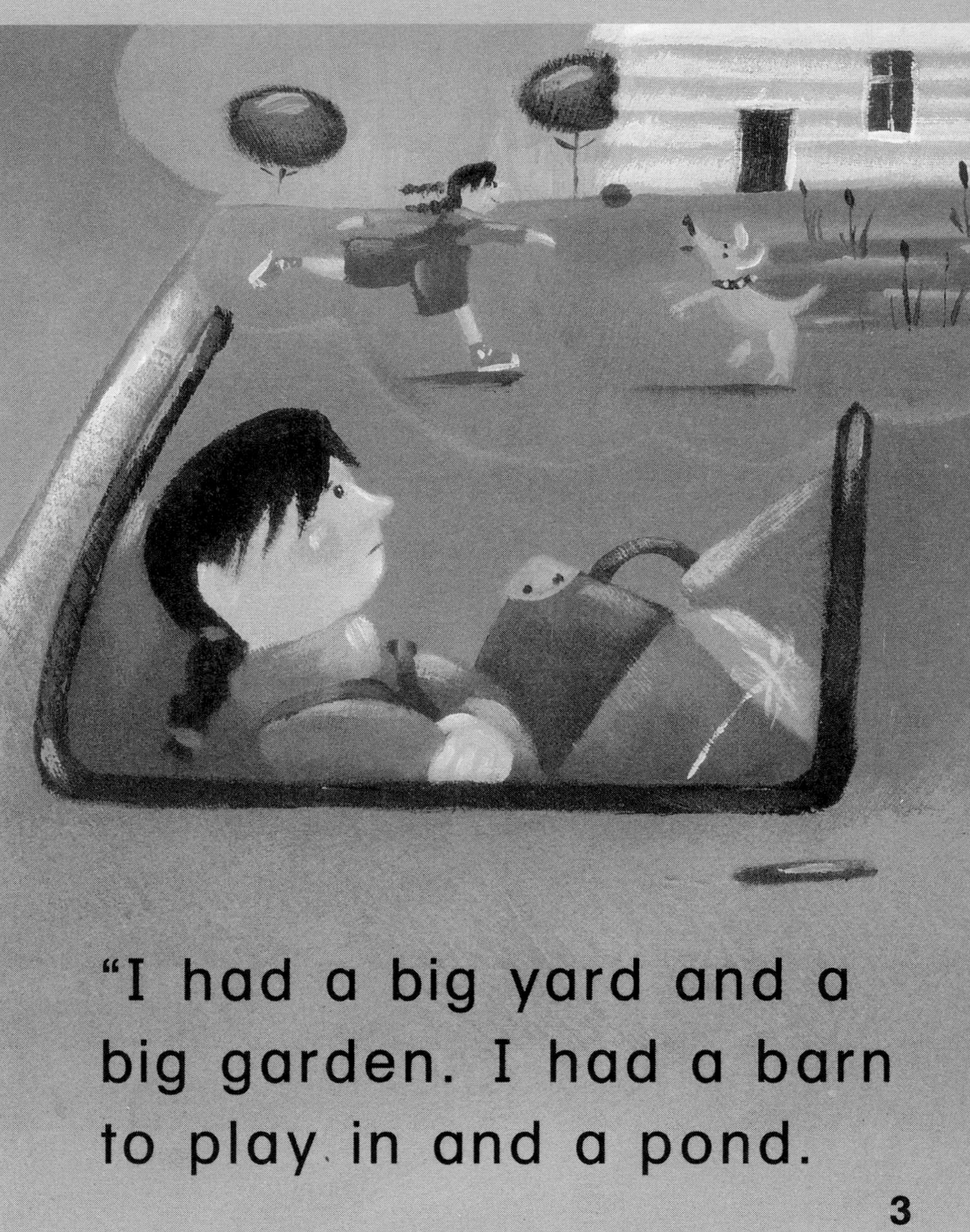

"I had a big yard and a big garden. I had a barn to play in and a pond.

"I could let Star run and bark. It's hard to do that here!

Fold

Back on the Farm

Word Count: 91

High-Frequency Words

could
do
good
here
like
play
said
the
to
too
was

Decodable Words*

a	**Carmen**	in	**park**
and	did	is	pond
arm	**far**	it's	run
back	**farm**	let	spot
bark	for	**marched**	**Star**
barn	**garden**	Mom	that
big	had	not	this
called	**hard**	off	wish
can	I	on	**yard**

*Words with /är/*ar* appear in **boldface** type.

"I like this park!"
said Carmen.
Star did, too.

Fold

"I wish I was back
on the farm!"

"Carmen," Mom called. "That is a good spot for a garden. Star can run in the park. It's not far."

Fold

Mom and Carmen marched off arm in arm.

DECODABLE BOOK 15
Zip! Zap! Quick!

Fold

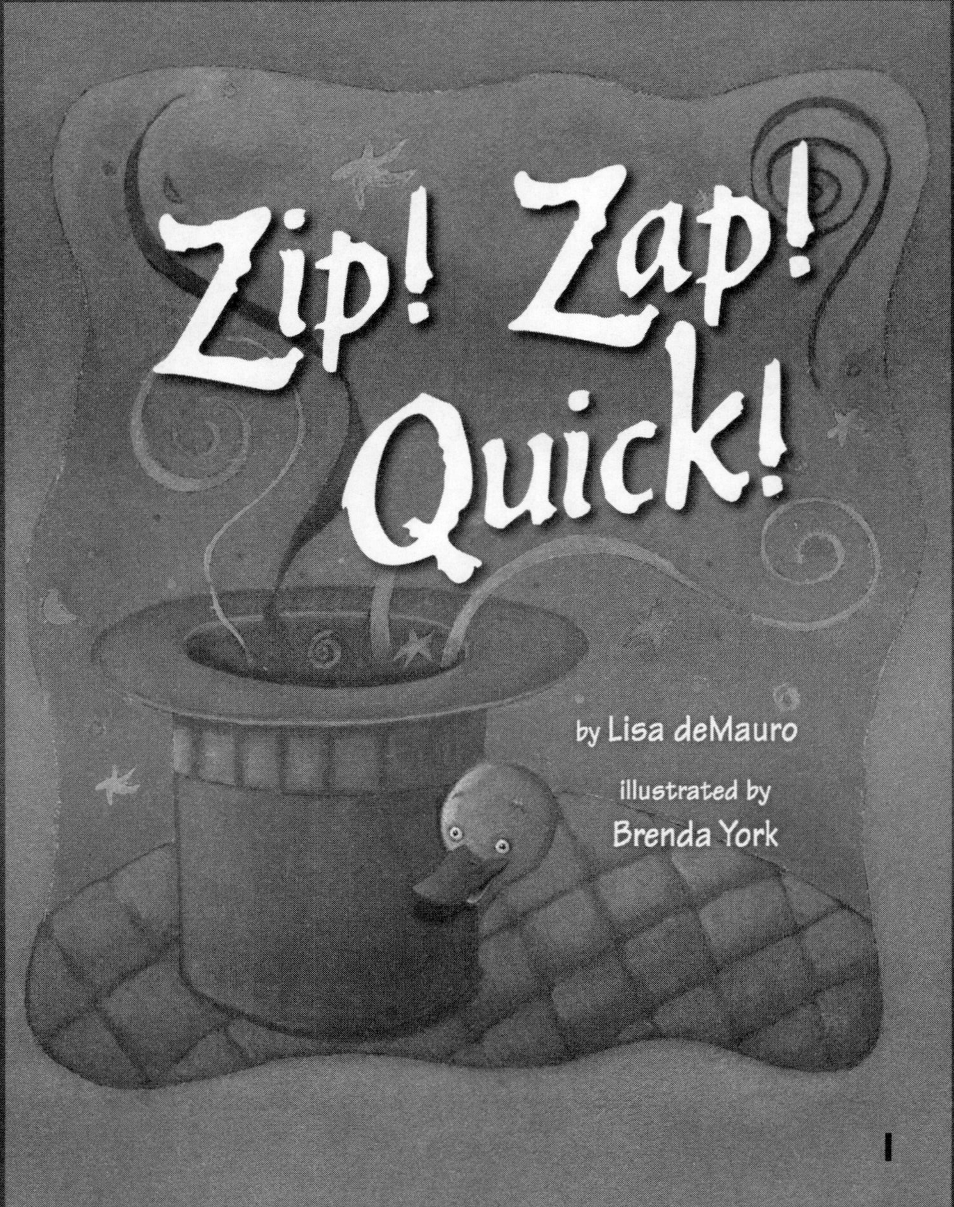

Zip! Zap! Quick!

by Lisa deMauro

illustrated by Brenda York

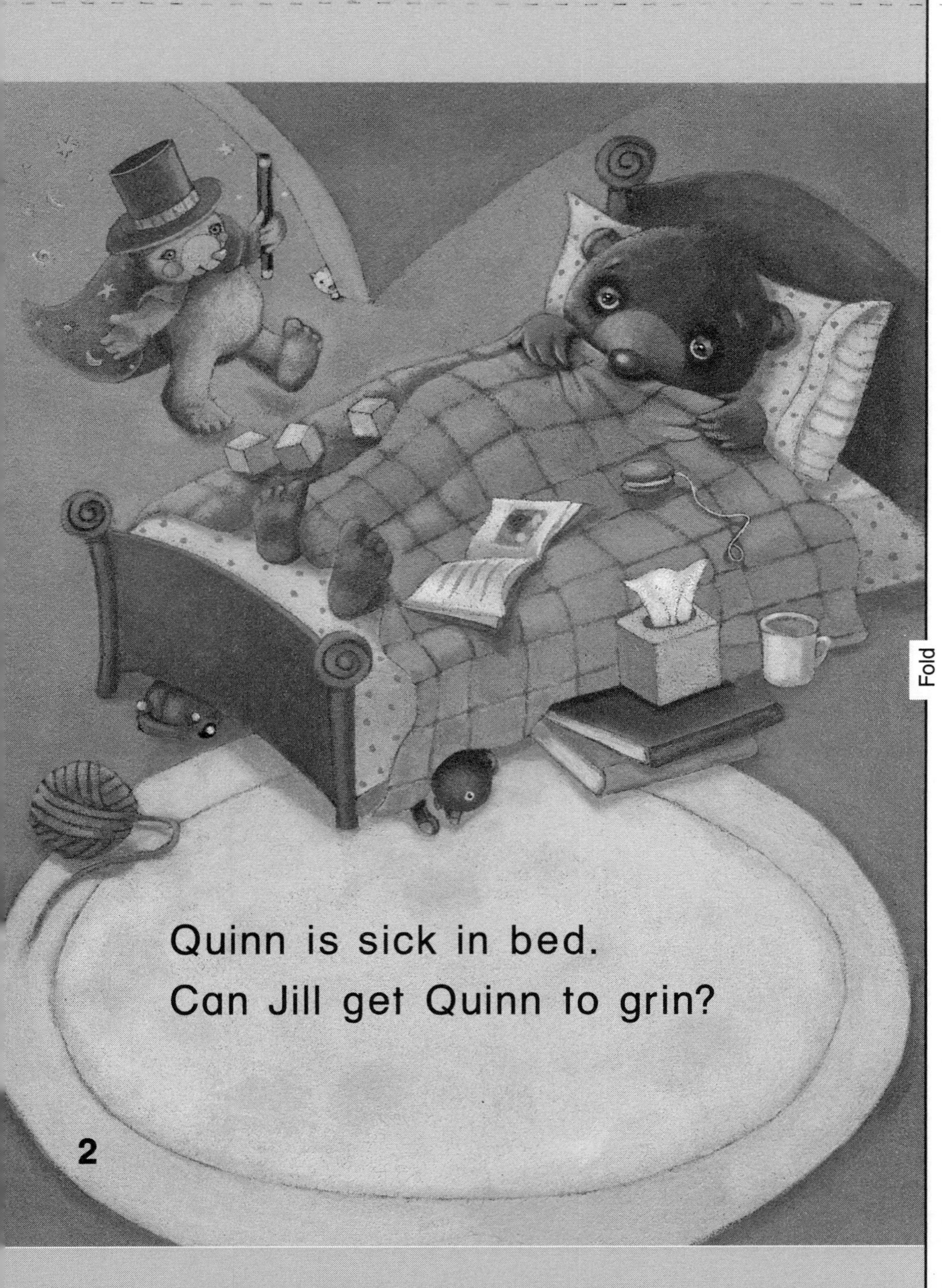

Quinn is sick in bed.
Can Jill get Quinn to grin?

Fold

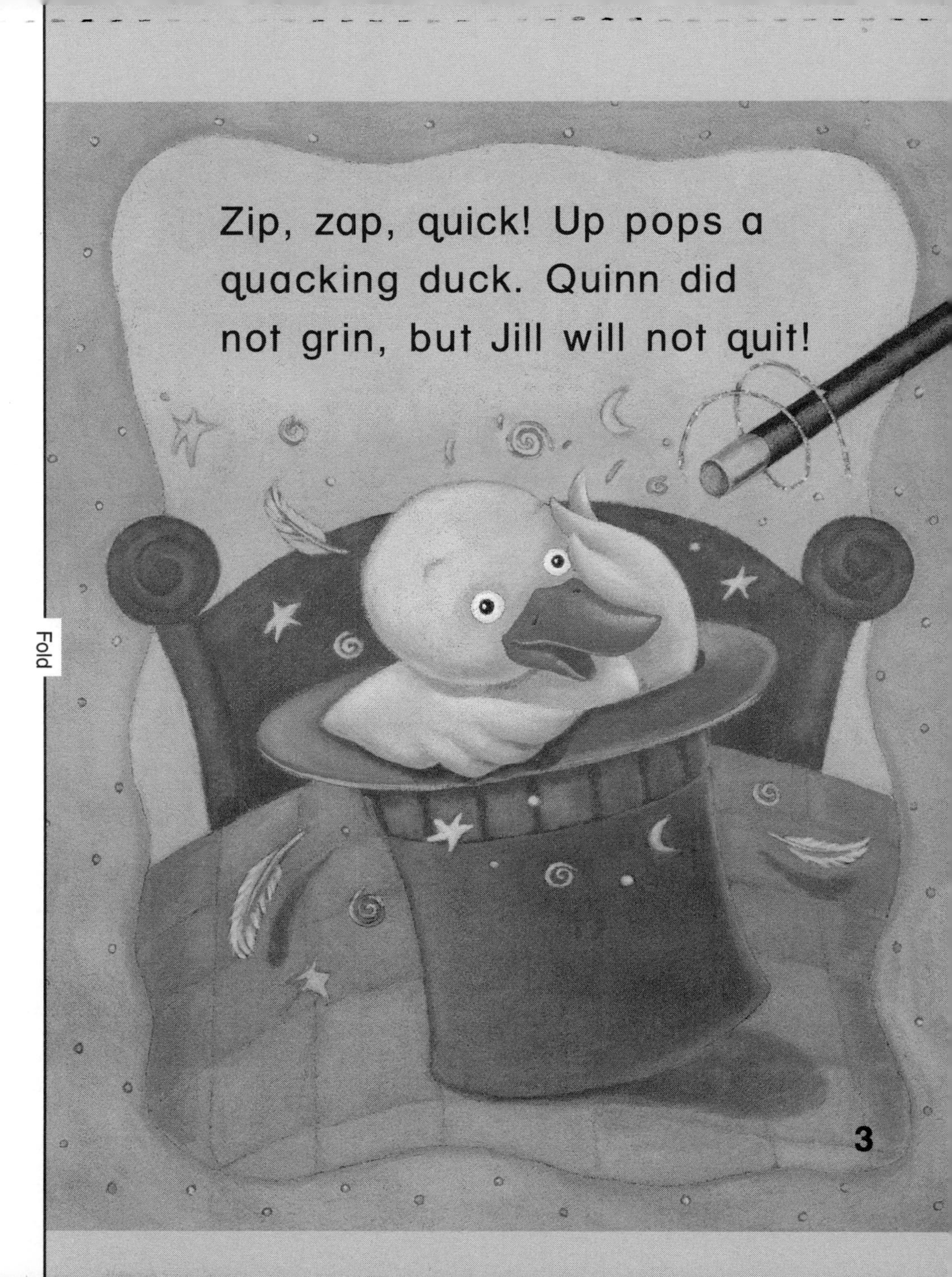

Zip, zap, quick! Up pops a quacking duck. Quinn did not grin, but Jill will not quit!

Fold

Jill sets a red car on Quinn's quilt. A scarf is on top. Will Quinn grin?

Fold

Zip! Zap! Quick!

Word Count: 111

High-Frequency Words

little
put
the
to

Decodable Words*

a	get	pops	sick
and	grin	**quacking**	spins
bed	has	**quacks**	top
big	in	**quick**	tugs
but	is	**quilt**	up
can	Jill	**Quinn**	will
car	Jill's	**Quinn's**	yarn
cup	kitten	**quit**	zap
did	not	red	zip
duck	off	scarf	
for	on	sets	

*Words with /kw/*qu* appear in **boldface** type.

Jill's kitten has the yarn!
Quinn has a big grin for Jill.
Quinn has a big, big grin
for Jill's kitten.

Fold

Zip, zap, quick! The car
is in Quinn's cup. Quinn
has a little grin, but Jill
will not quit!

Jill has put yarn on Quinn's quilt. Quinn tugs and tugs. The yarn spins off the quilt. "Quick!" quacks the duck. "Get Jill's yarn!"

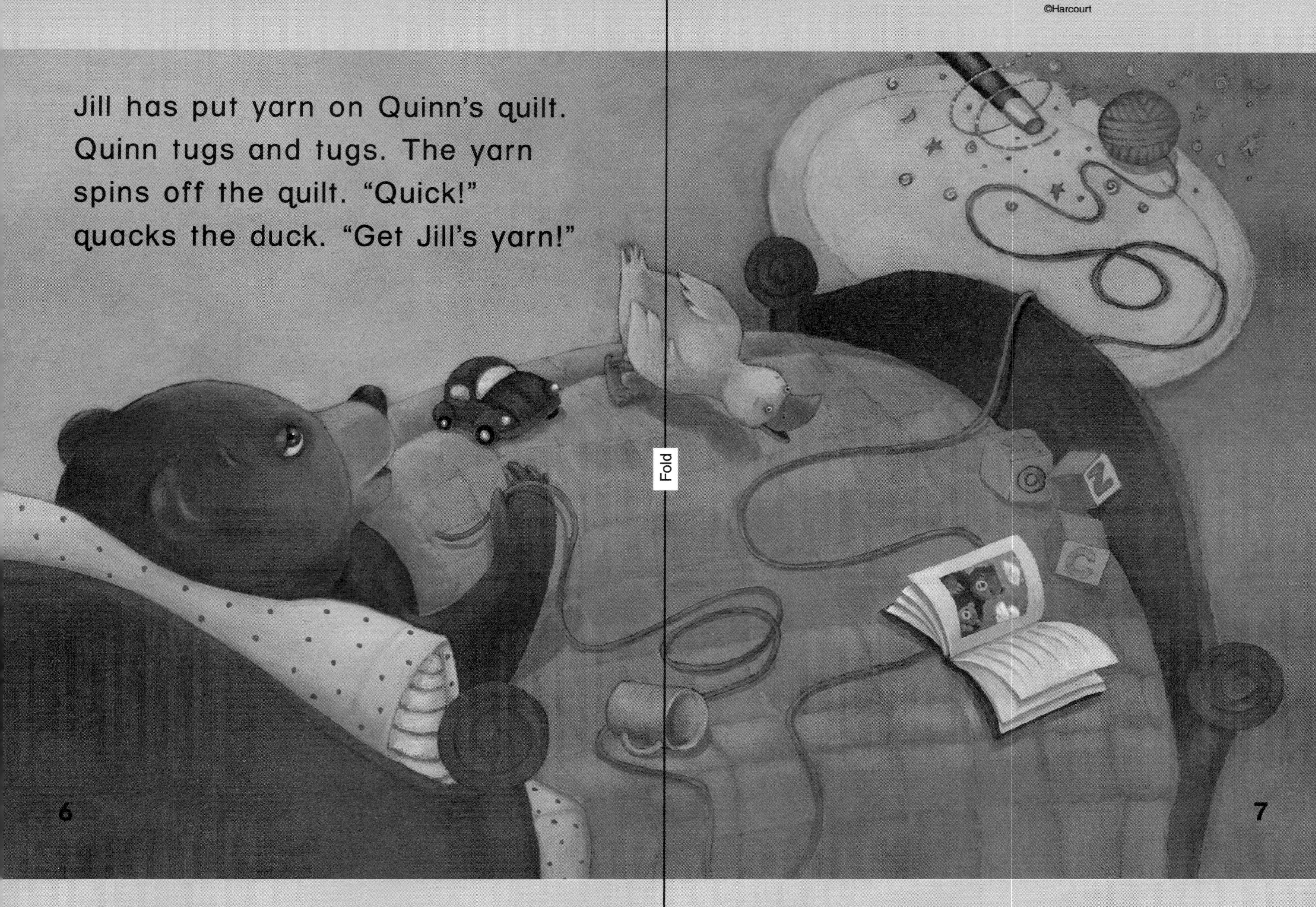

Fold

DECODABLE BOOK 15
The Whiz

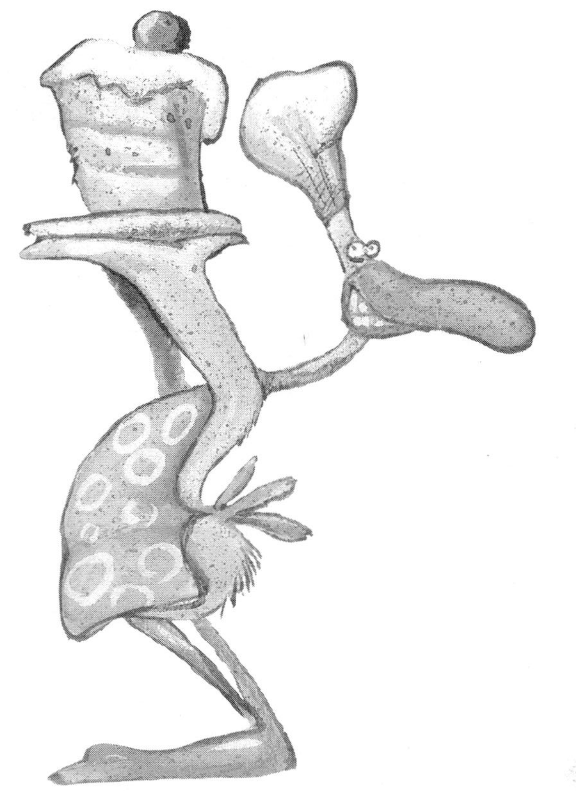

Fold

The Whiz

by J.C. Cunningham
illustrated by Gary Bialke

Pig was sick.
Duck went to visit him.

Fold

Fold

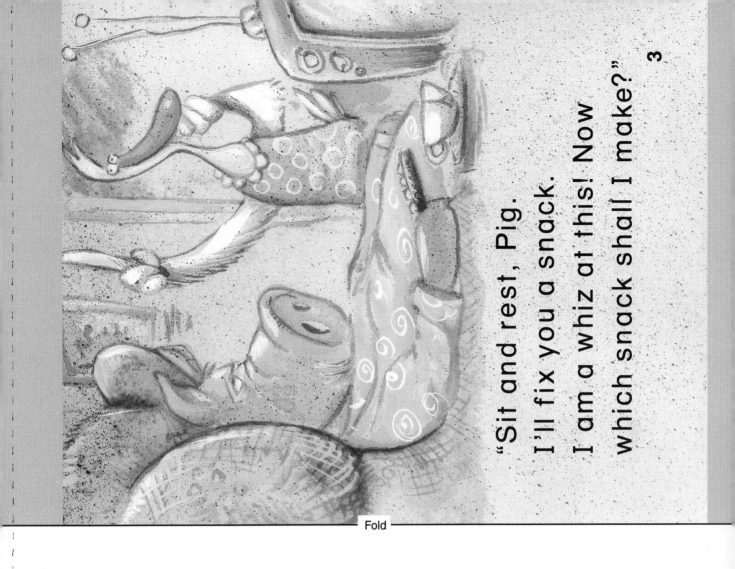

"Sit and rest, Pig.
I'll fix you a snack.
I am a whiz at this! Now
which snack shall I make?"

Duck started to chop up plums. Whack! Whack! Whack! "Sit and rest, Pig. I'll whip this up in no time!"

Fold

The Whiz

Word Count: 90

High-Frequency Words

comes	what
have	you
here	
make	
no	
now	
she	
the	
time	
to	
was	

Decodable Words*

a	fix	shall	visit
am	him	sick	went
and	I	sit	**whack**
at	I'll	smash	**wham**
bam	in	snack	**when**
bang	it	snacks	**which**
champ	mess	snorted	**whiff**
chop	mixed	started	**whip**
crash	Pig	this	**whiz**
Duck	plums	tossed	
eggs	rest	up	

*Words with /hw/*wh* appear in **boldface** type.

“What a whiz,” snorted Pig,
“and what a mess!”

Fold

Duck mixed and mixed.
Bam! Crash! Bang!
She tossed in eggs.
Wham! Wham!

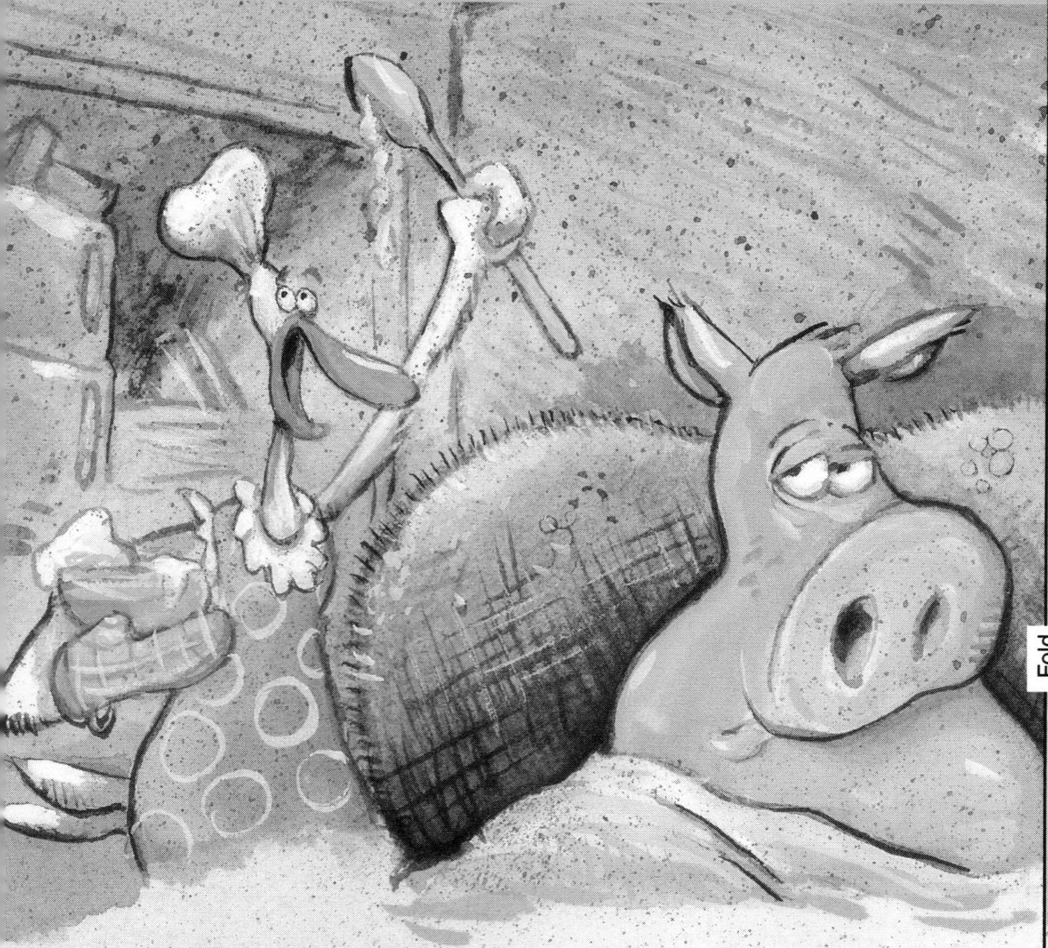

“When it comes to snacks,
I am the champ!” Whack!
Smash! Wham!

Fold

“Here, Pig! Have a whiff!”

DECODABLE BOOK 15
"Quick!" Barked the King

Fold

"Quick!" Barked the King

by Max Saal

illustrated by John Ceballos

"Let's play," barked Quint.
"I'll act like a king."
"OK," Quill barked.

Fold

Quint wore a big red quilt.
He looked just like a king.

Fold

"Quill!" barked King Quint.
"Quick! Quack like a duck."

Fold

"Quick!" Barked the King

Word Count: 85

High-Frequency Words

don't
he
like
looked
no
now
oh
play
the

Decodable Words*

a	just	**Quint**
act	king	**quit**
and	let's	ran
barked	OK	red
big	**quack**	run
duck	**quacked**	this
fun	**quacking**	will
I	**quick**	wore
I'll	**Quill**	yelled
is	**quilt**	

*Words with /kw/*qu* appear in **boldface** type.

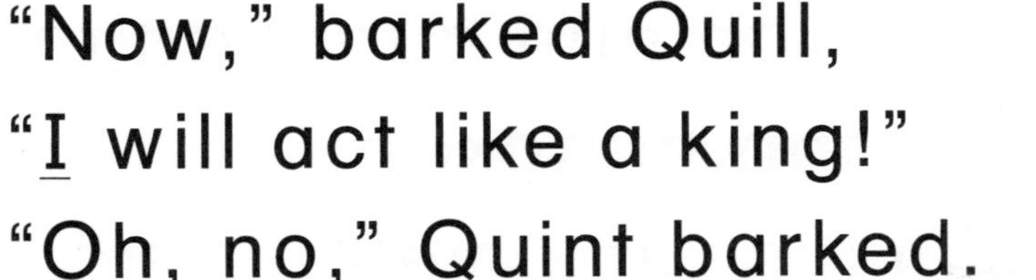

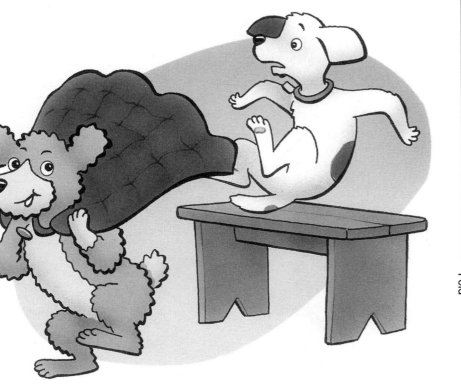

"Now," barked Quill,
"I will act like a king!"
"Oh, no," Quint barked.

Fold

Quill quacked like a duck.
"Quack, quack, quack!"

“Quill!” King Quint barked.
“Quick! Now run like a duck
and don’t quit quacking!”

Fold

Quill ran and quacked and
ran and quacked.
“This is fun!” yelled Quint.

DECODABLE BOOK 15
Cluck! Quack! Wham! Whack!

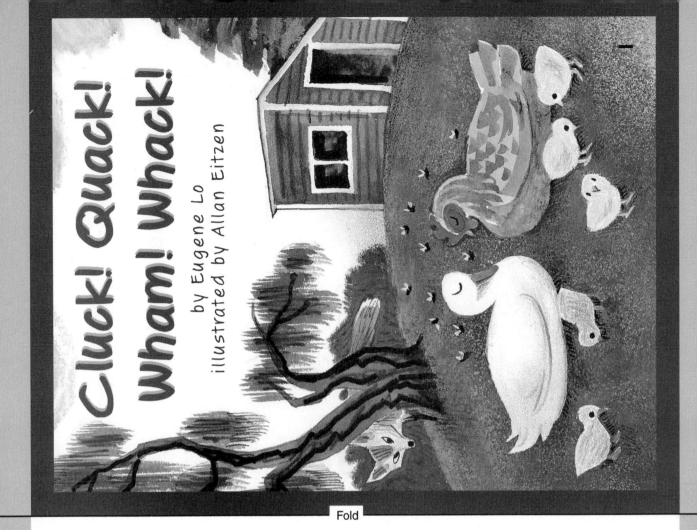

Fold

Cluck! Quack! Wham! Whack!

by Eugene Lo
illustrated by Allan Eitzen

Bugs whiz and buzz.
"Hmmm," clucks Hen.
"Which bug shall I
pick for a snack?"

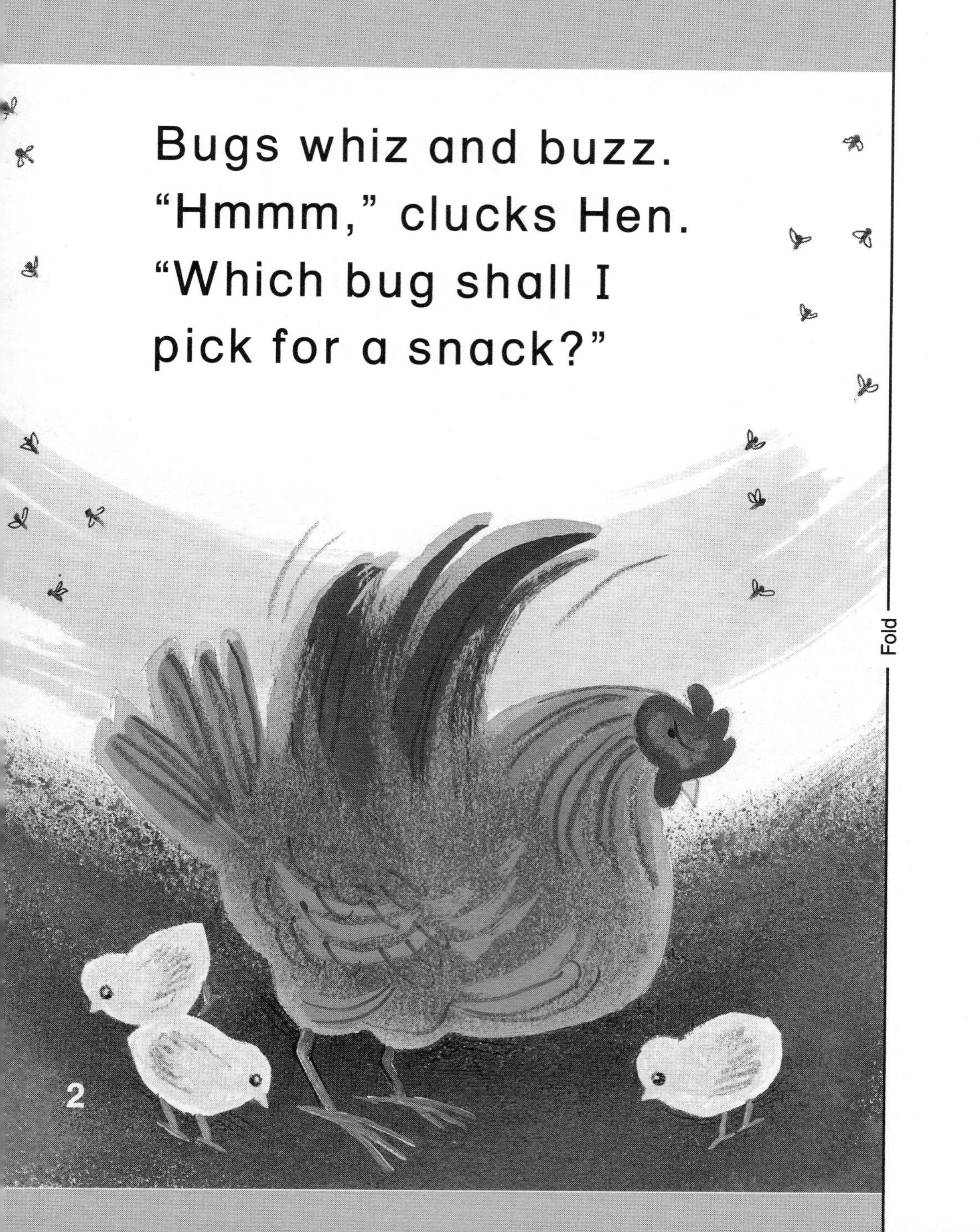

Fold

Fold

Hen is not quick, and the bugs whiz off. When Hen naps, the bugs come back.

Bugs whiz and buzz.
"Hmmm," quacks Duck.
"Which bug shall I pick
for a snack?"

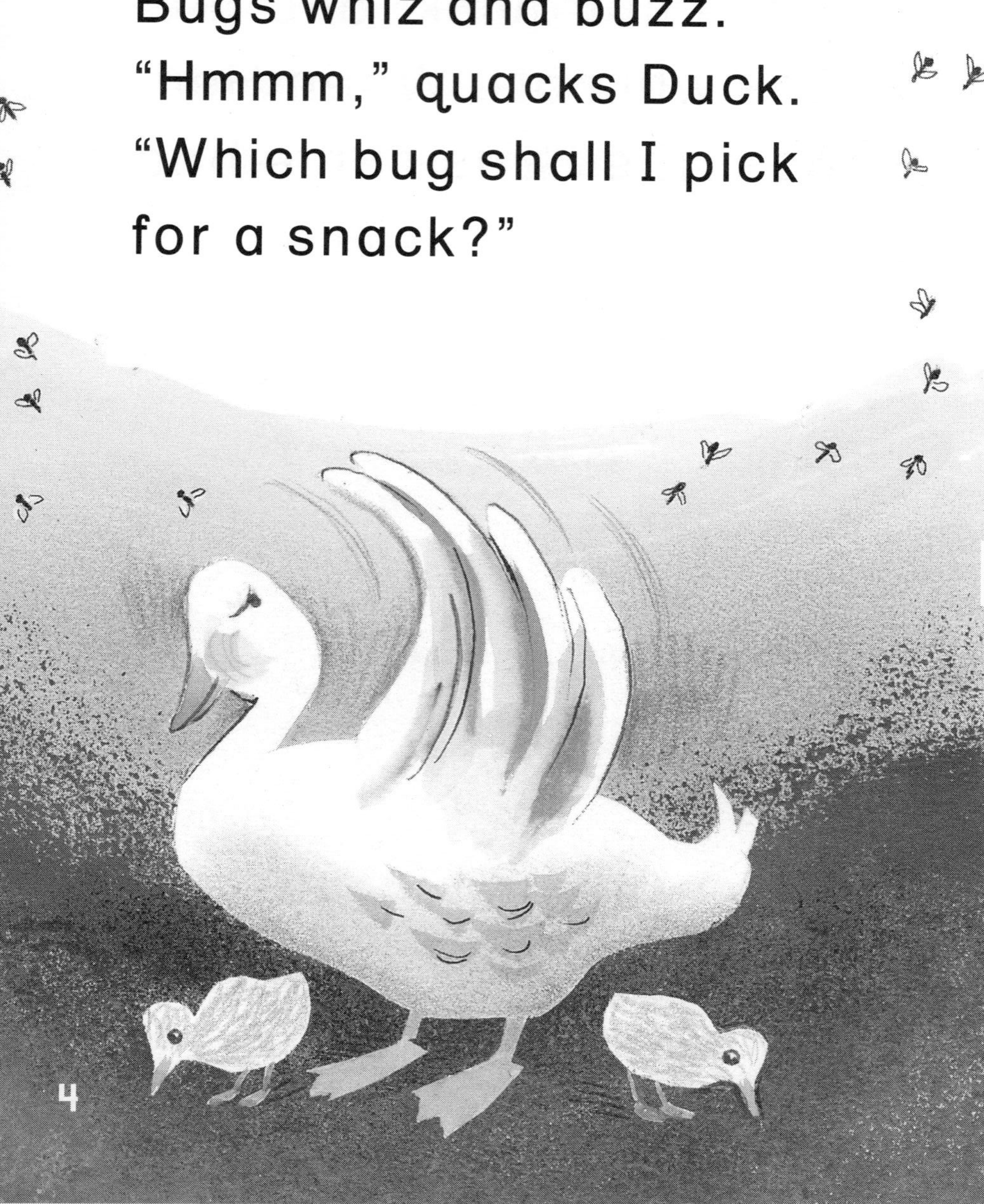

Fold

Cluck! Quack! Wham! Whack!

Word Count: 98

High-Frequency Words

come
he
of
the

Decodable Words*

a	hmmm	thinks
and	I	trots
back	is	**whack**
bug	naps	**wham**
bugs	not	**when**
buzz	off	**which**
cluck	pick	**whiff**
clucks	quack	**whiz**
Duck	quacks	will
for	quick	
Fox	shall	
gets	snack	
Hen	sniff	

*Words with /hw/*wh* appear in **boldface** type.

Cluck! Quack! Wham!
Whack! Off trots Fox.
He will not come back!

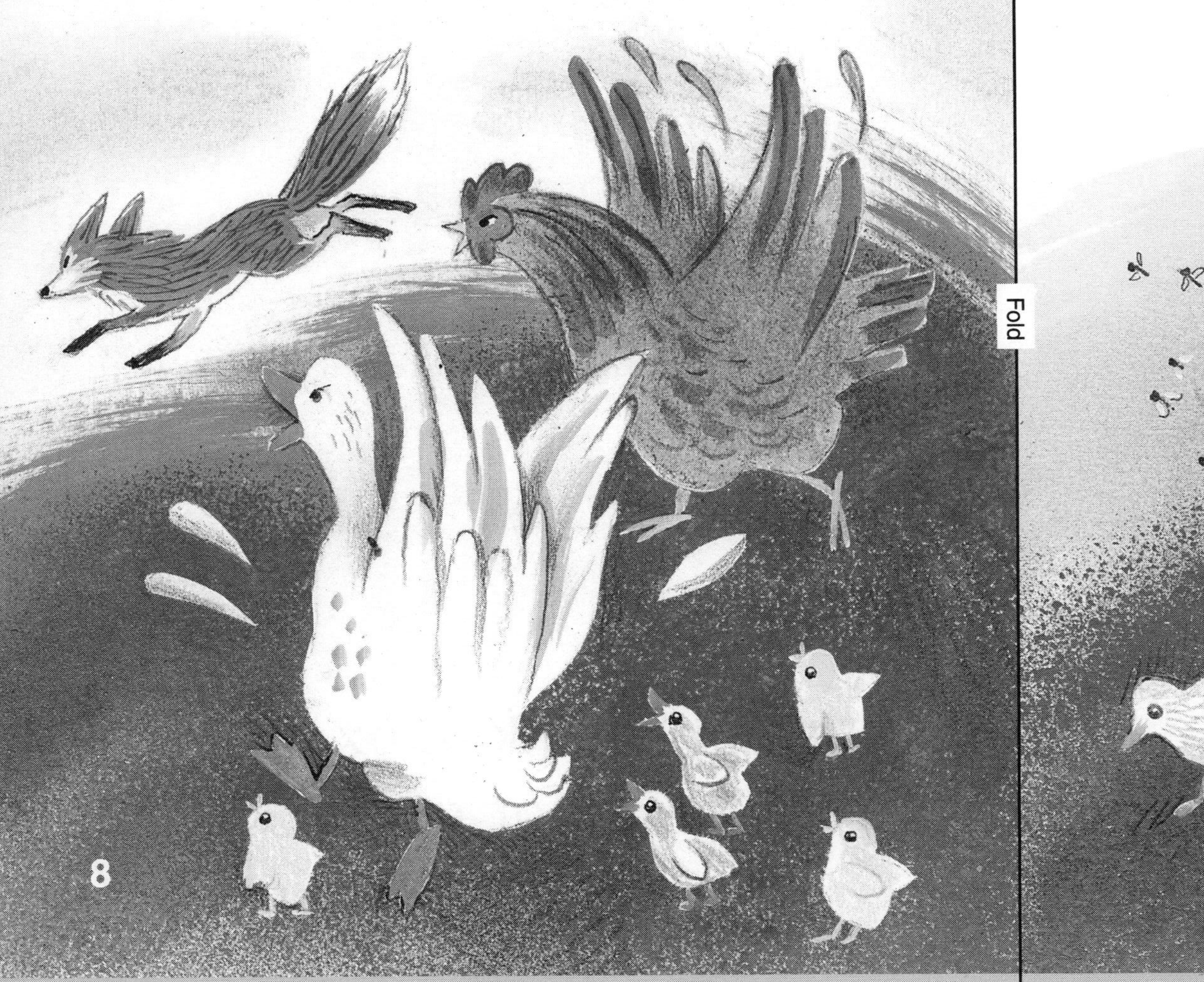

Fold

Duck is not quick, and the bugs whiz off. When Duck naps, the bugs come back.

Sniff, sniff. Fox gets a whiff of Hen and Duck.

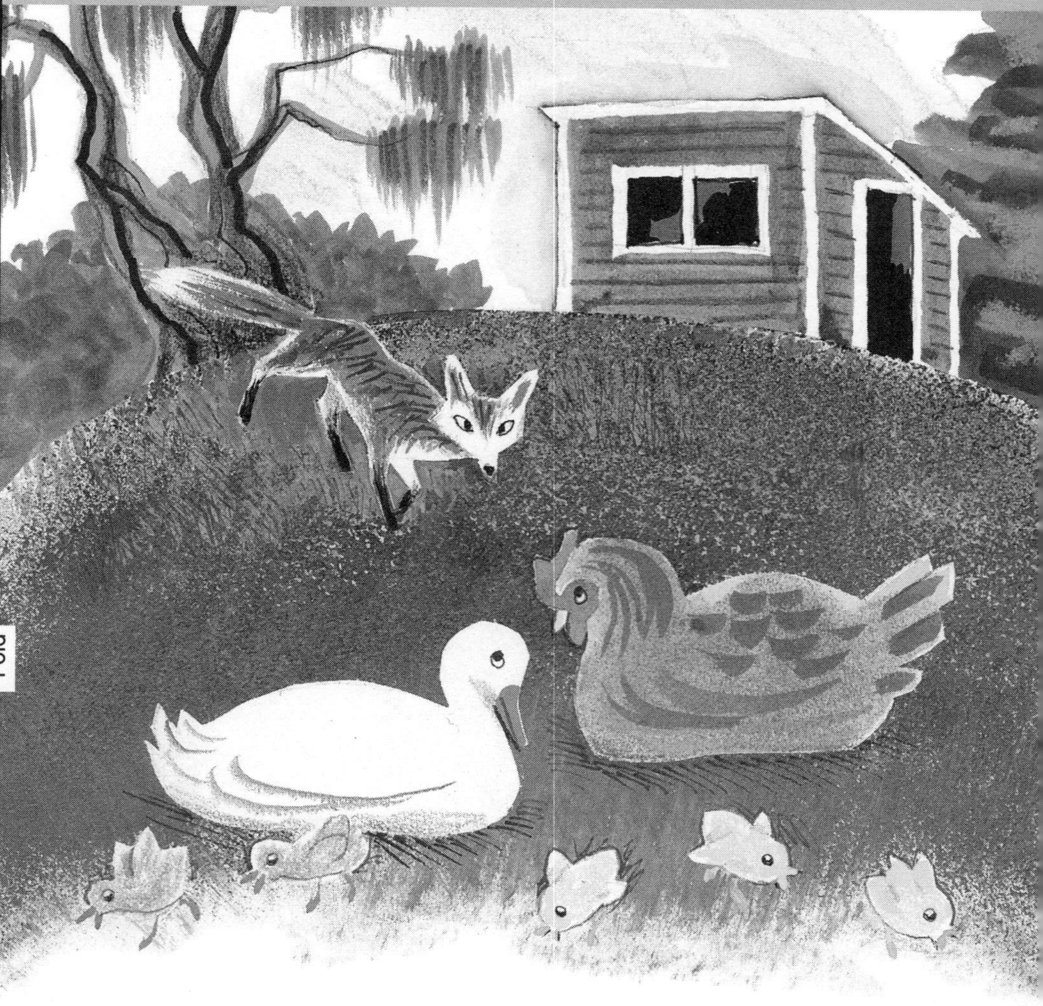

Fold

"Hmmm," thinks Fox. "Which shall I pick for a snack?"

DECODABLE BOOK 16
Dr. Kern

Fold

Dr. Kern

by Ruth Rogg
illustrated by Lizzy Rockwell

Gert is sick. Mom and Gert must visit Dr. Kern.

Fold

Fold

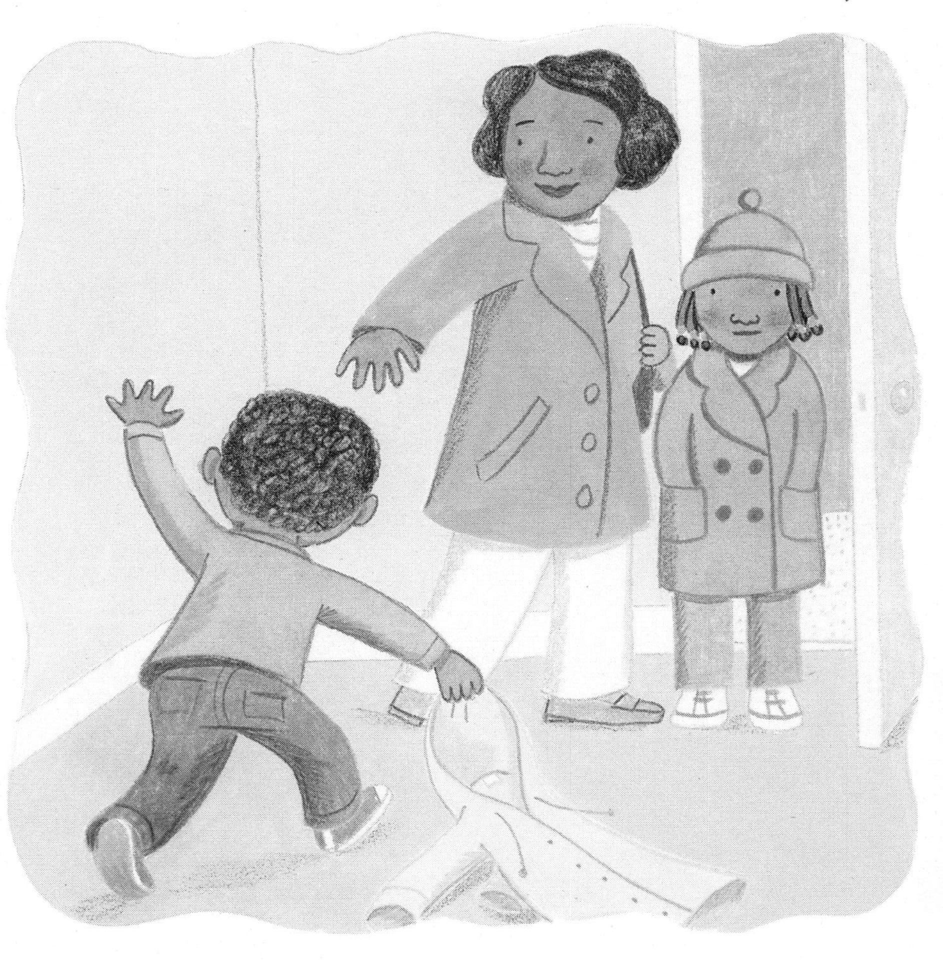

Sherm runs after them.
"Me, too!" Sherm calls.

Dr. Kern is stern as she checks Gert. Sherm looks stern, too.

Fold

Dr. Kern

Word Count: 89

High-Frequency Words

be
gives
grow
like
looks
me
she
soon
to
too
you

Decodable Words*

a
after
and
as
bed
better
calls
checks
Dr.
Gert
get
grins
her
hug
hugs
I
in
is
just
Kern
Mom
must
rest
runs
Sherm
sick
stern
tells
them
then
up
visit
when
will

*Words with /ûr/*er* appear in **boldface** type.

"When I grow up," Sherm tells Dr. Kern, "I will be a doctor, just like you!"

Fold

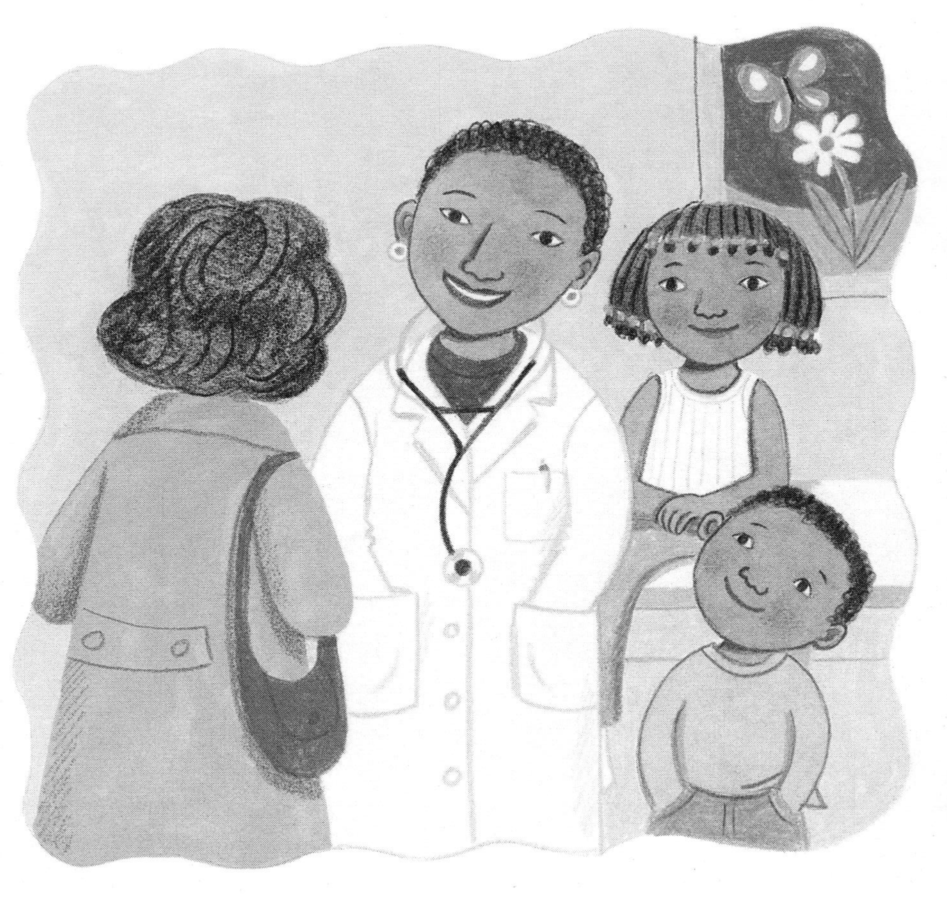

"Gert will get better soon," Dr. Kern tells Mom. Then she grins. Sherm grins, too.

Dr. Kern tells Gert to rest
in bed. Then Dr. Kern
gives her a hug.

Fold

"Me, too!" Sherm calls.
Dr. Kern grins and
hugs Sherm, too.

DECODABLE BOOK 16

The Third Bird

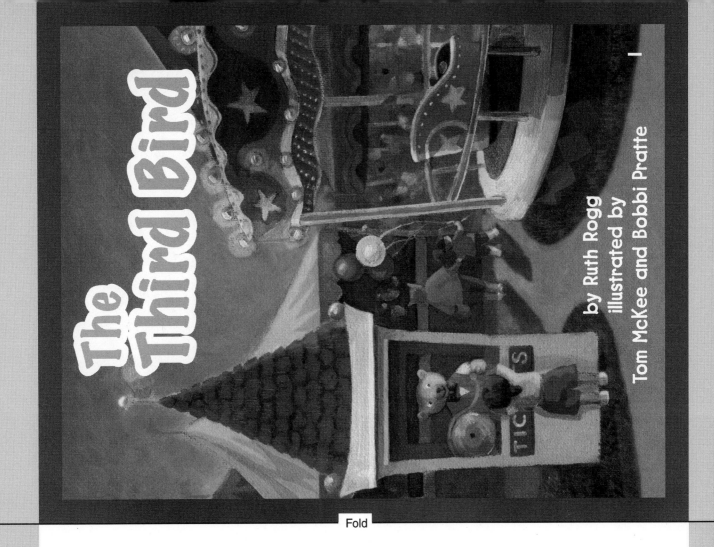

Fold

The Third Bird

by Ruth Rogg

illustrated by

Tom McKee and Bobbi Pratte

Shirl and Gram had fun
on the Whirl-and-Twirl.

Fold

Fold

Then Shirl saw a big, red bird.
"I must win that bird!" Shirl said.

"Hit the little birds and make them swirl," said Kirk. "No one can do it. Can you?"

Fold

The Third Bird

Word Count: 104

High-Frequency Words

do	no
everyone	one
give	said
go	saw
little	the
make	want
my	you

Decodable Words*

a	had	**sir**
and	held	**squirt**
big	her	**swirl**
bird	hit	that
birds	I	them
but	it	then
can	**Kirk**	**third**
did	let	**twirl**
first	must	**whirl**
fun	next	win
girl	on	yelled
got	red	yes
Gram	**Shirl**	

*Words with /ûr/*ir* appear in **boldface** type.

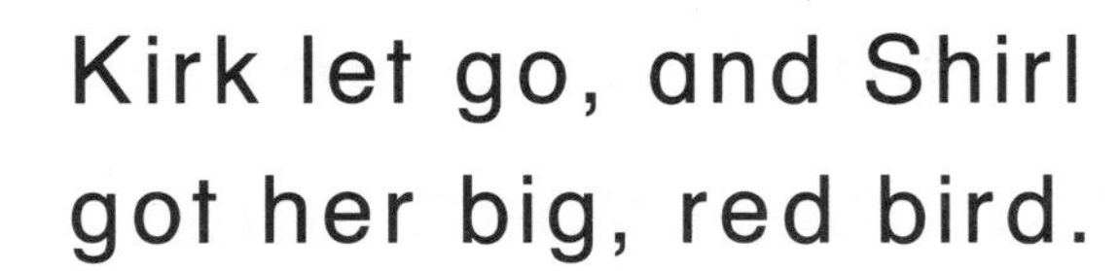

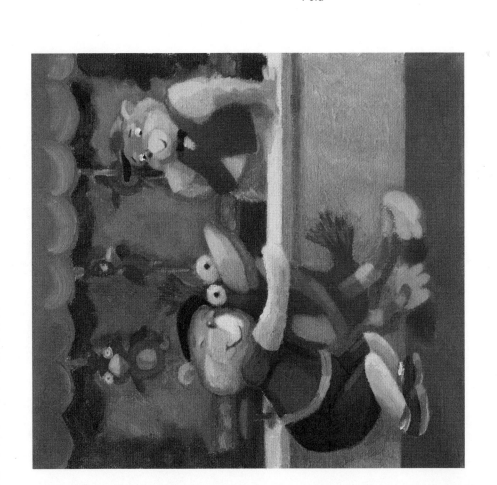

Kirk let go, and Shirl got her big, red bird.

Fold

"Yes, sir!" said Shirl. "Yes, I can!" Squirt! Shirl hit the first bird. Squirt! Shirl hit the next bird.

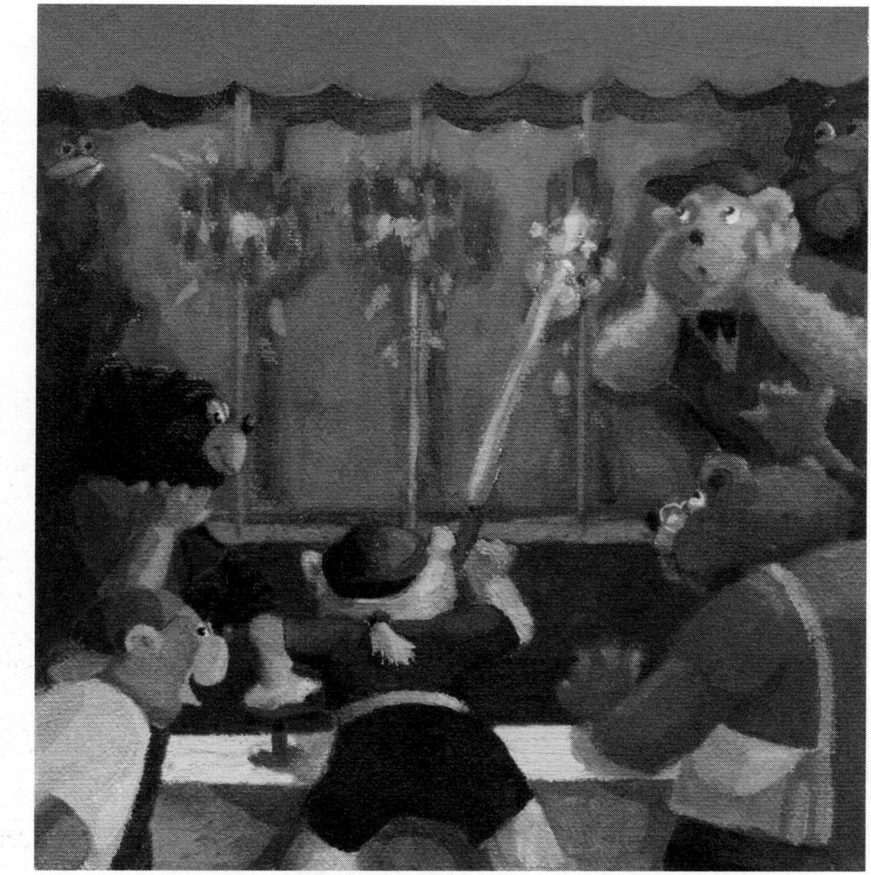

Squirt! Shirl hit the third bird!
"That little girl did it!"
yelled Kirk.

Fold

"I want my red bird," Shirl said, but Kirk held on. "Give her the red bird!" everyone said.

DECODABLE BOOK 16
Burt and Curtis

Fold

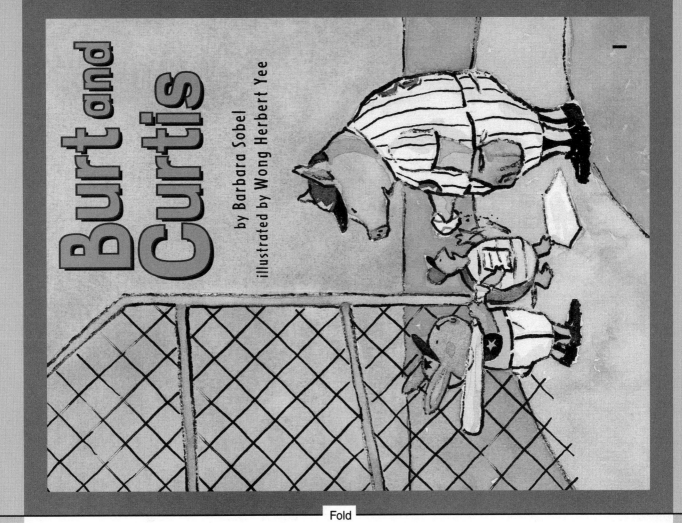

Burt and Curtis

by Barbara Sobel
illustrated by Wong Herbert Yee

Burt is the batter.
Curtis is the pitcher.

Fold

Curtis turns and picks up the ball. “I can hit that ball,” Burt thinks. “I can do it.”

Fold

“Burt can’t hit this ball,” Curtis thinks. “I’ll toss a curve ball.”

Fold

Burt and Curtis

Word Count: 103

High-Frequency Words

by
do
he
looks
now
so
the

Decodable Words*

a
and
as
ball
batter
blur
burns
Burt
Burt’s
can
can’t
curl
Curtis
curve
fast
flashes
fur
grins
hit
hurls
I
I’ll
in
is
it
misses
picks
pitcher
runs
scores
sobs
swings
that
thinks
this
toss
turf
turns
up
whack
whir
whiz
will

*Words with /ûr/*ur* appear in **boldface** type.

Burt burns up the turf as he runs and scores. Now Burt grins and Curtis sobs!

Fold

Curtis hurls the ball.
Burt swings and misses.

Curtis grins and Burt sobs. "Now I'll toss a fast ball," Curtis thinks. "It will whiz by so fast that Burt's fur will curl!"

Fold

Whack! Whir! Curtis looks up, up, up. The ball flashes by in a blur.

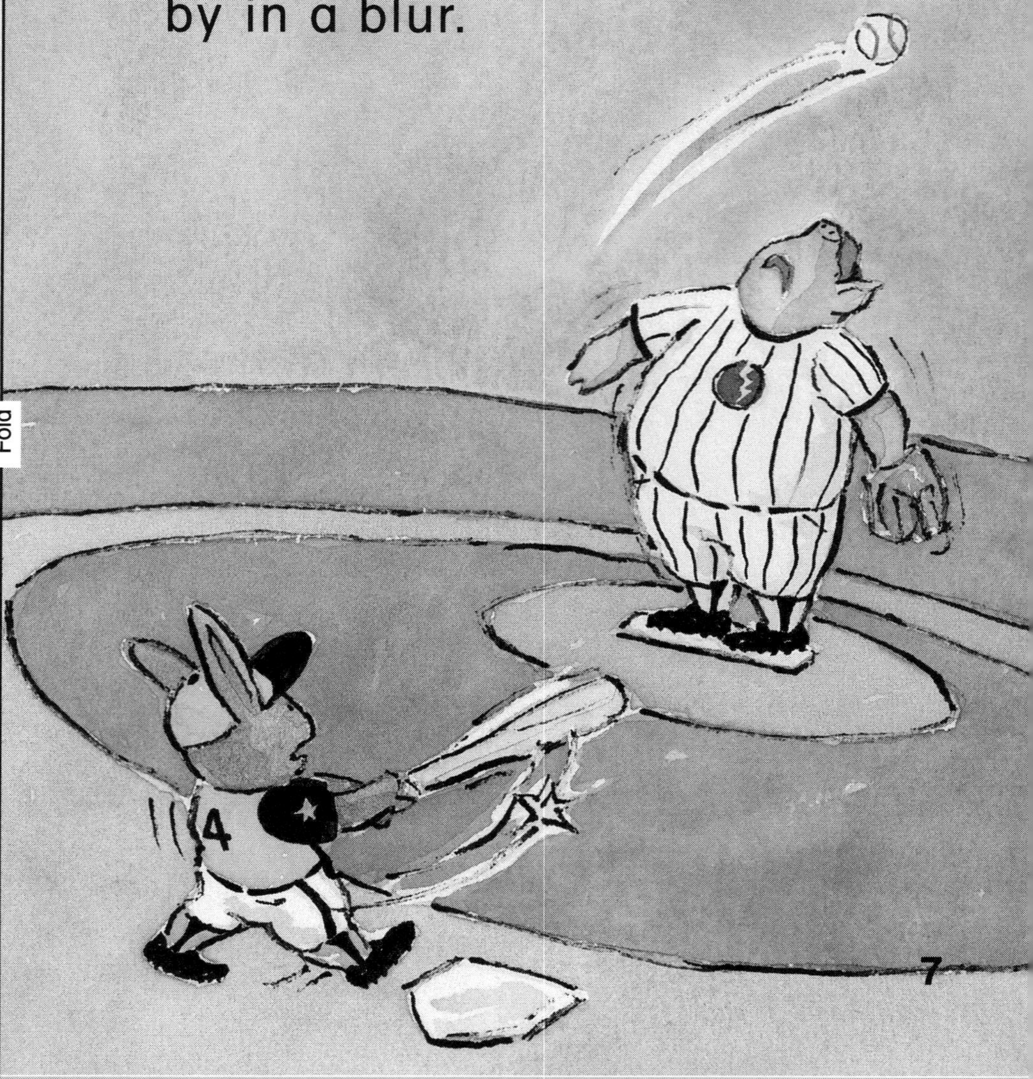

DECODABLE BOOK 16
Mom's Helper

Fold

Mom's Helper

by Kathleen McKinnon
illustrated by Laura Rader

I help Mom. I am her helper.

Fold

Fold

I help fix dinner. I mix things. Mom tells me that I am the best mixer.

I help Mom in the garden.
I help her with the plants.

Fold

Mom's Helper

Word Count: 96

High-Frequency Words

don't
give
likes
me
needs
the
to
too

Decodable Words*

a	garden	jump	plants
am	help	let	rest
and	**helper**	mix	tells
best	**her**	**mixer**	that
but	**Herb**	Mom	things
dig	him	Mom's	tub
digger	hug	nap	when
dinner	I	**napper**	with
dog	in	**perfect**	
fix	**jerk**	plant	

*Words with /ûr/*er* appear in **boldface** type.

I nap, too. Mom tells me that I am a perfect napper!

Fold

When I plant, I dig. Mom tells me that I am the best digger.

I help Mom with Herb. That dog likes to jump and jerk in the tub, but I don't let him.

Fold

When Mom needs a rest, I help her. I give her a hug.

DECODABLE BOOK 16
Dig and Stir

Fold

Fern sat in the dirt.
All she did was dig and stir.
Dig and stir.
Dig and stir.

Fold

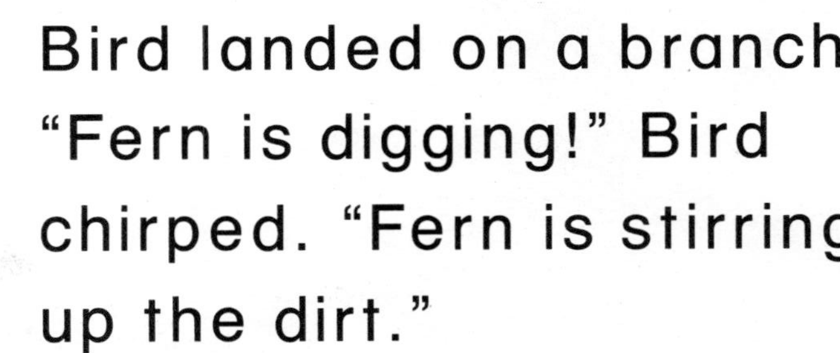

Fold

Bird landed on a branch. “Fern is digging!” Bird chirped. “Fern is stirring up the dirt.”

Fern was thinking, "This dirt is too firm. Soon this dirt will be just right."

Fold

Dig and Stir

Word Count: 97

High-Frequency Words

be
like
make
right
she
soon
the
too
was

Decodable Words*

a
all
and
bird
birds
branch
bugs
chirped
did
dig
digging
dirt
Fern
firm
first
garden
gardens
grinned
I
in
is
it
just
landed
next
on
plant
planted
sang
sat
stir
stirring
swirl
thinking
third
this
twirl
up
whirl
will
winked
yum

Words with /ûr/*ir* appear in **boldface** type.

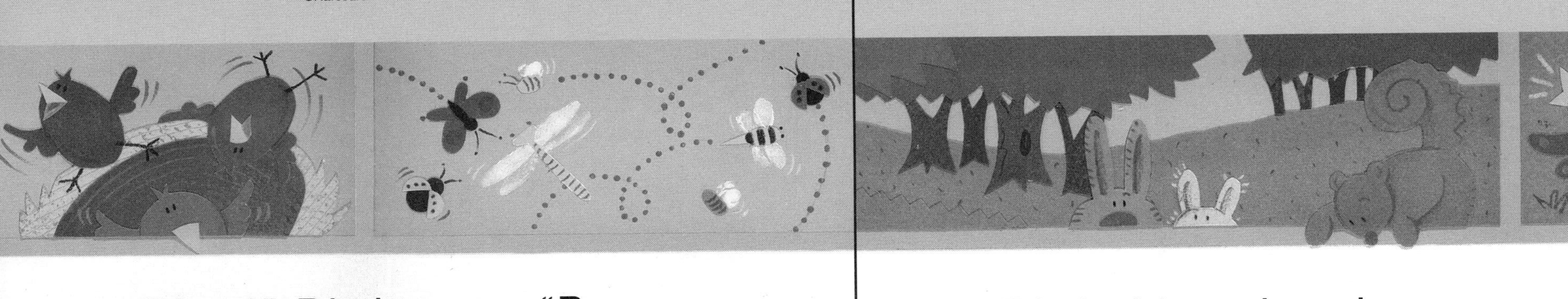

"Yum!" Bird sang. "Bugs like gardens. Birds like bugs!" Fern just grinned.

Fold

Bird chirped and sang,
"Dig, stir. Whirl, twirl.
Stir the dirt. Make it swirl."

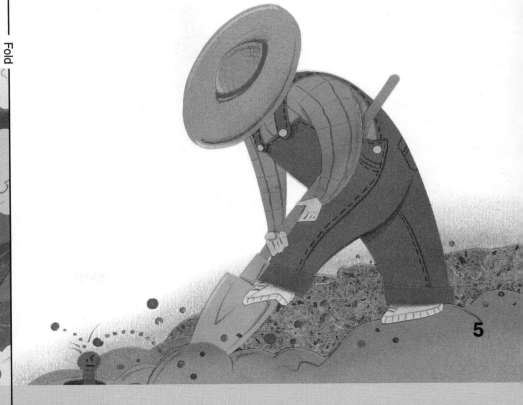

Fern winked. "First, I dig.
Next, I stir. Third, I plant!"

Fold

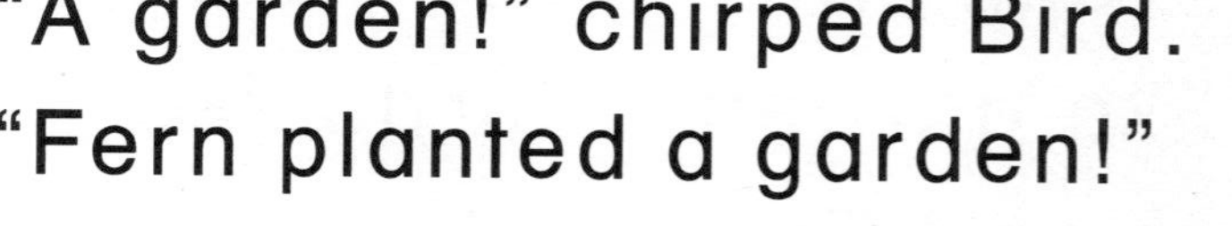

"A garden!" chirped Bird.
"Fern planted a garden!"

DECODABLE BOOK 16
Burk's Sunburn

Fold

Burk's Sunburn

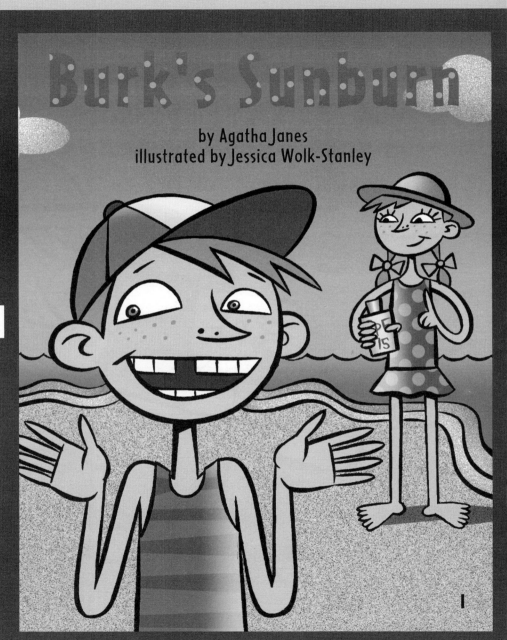

by Agatha Janes
illustrated by Jessica Wolk-Stanley

Burk and Kim were at the shore. “Burk,” Kim called, “rub this on or you will get a sunburn.”

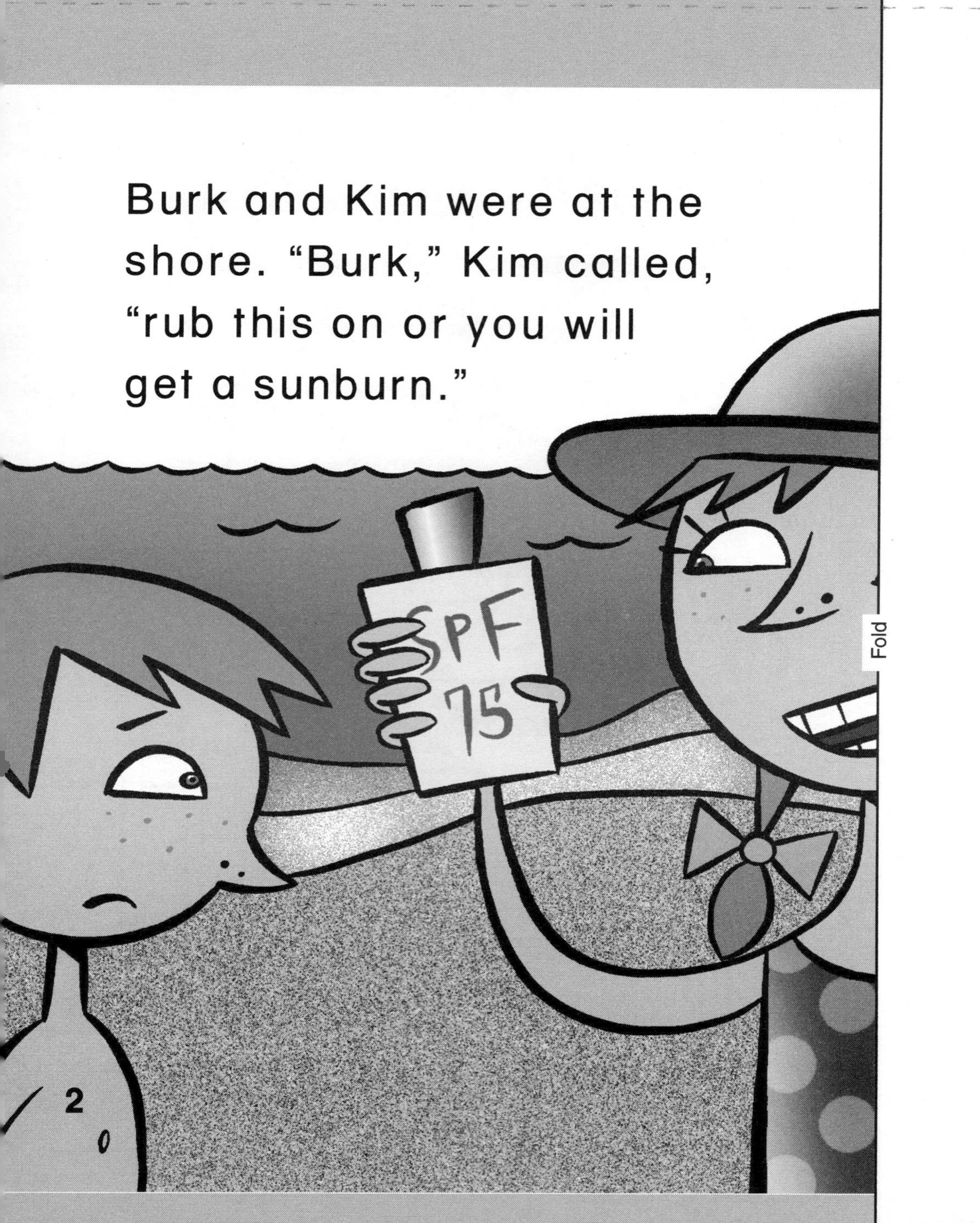

Fold

“I’m OK,” said Burk. Then he turned and ran into the surf.

Fold

The surf churned and swirled. Burk had so much fun. Burk was such a good swimmer.

Fold

Burk's Sunburn

Word Count: 100

High-Frequency Words

are
be
day
do
good
he
into
looked
now
said
so
the
to
was
were
what
you

Decodable Words*

a
and
at
big
Burk
Burk's
burnt
called
churned
crisp
forgot
fun
get
had
him
his
hurts
I'm
it
Kim
much
never
not
OK
on
or
pink
ran
red
rub
shore
sister
skin
such
sunburn
surf
swimmer
swirled
tells
that
then
this
turned
turning
will
yelled

*Words with /ûr/*ur* appear in **boldface** type.

Burk never forgot that day.
Now Burk will do what his
big sister tells him.

Fold

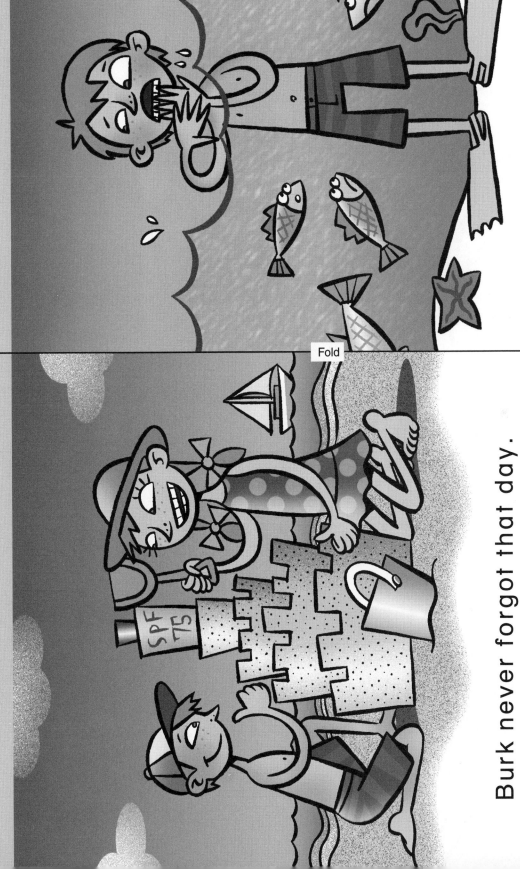

Then Burk looked at his skin.
It was turning red! Sunburn!

"I'm red!" Burk yelled. "It hurts! I'm burnt to a crisp!"

"You are pink, not red," said Kim. "Rub this on. It will be OK."

DECODABLE BOOK 17
A Picnic for Winkle

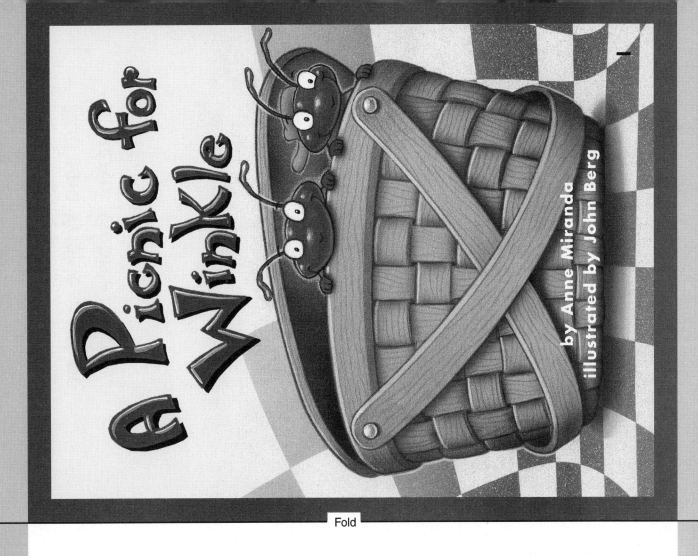

Fold

A Picnic for Winkle

by Anne Miranda
illustrated by John Berg

Dad and Winkle went on a picnic. Gobble, nibble.

Fold

Winkle gobbled up chips.
Dad nibbled an apple.

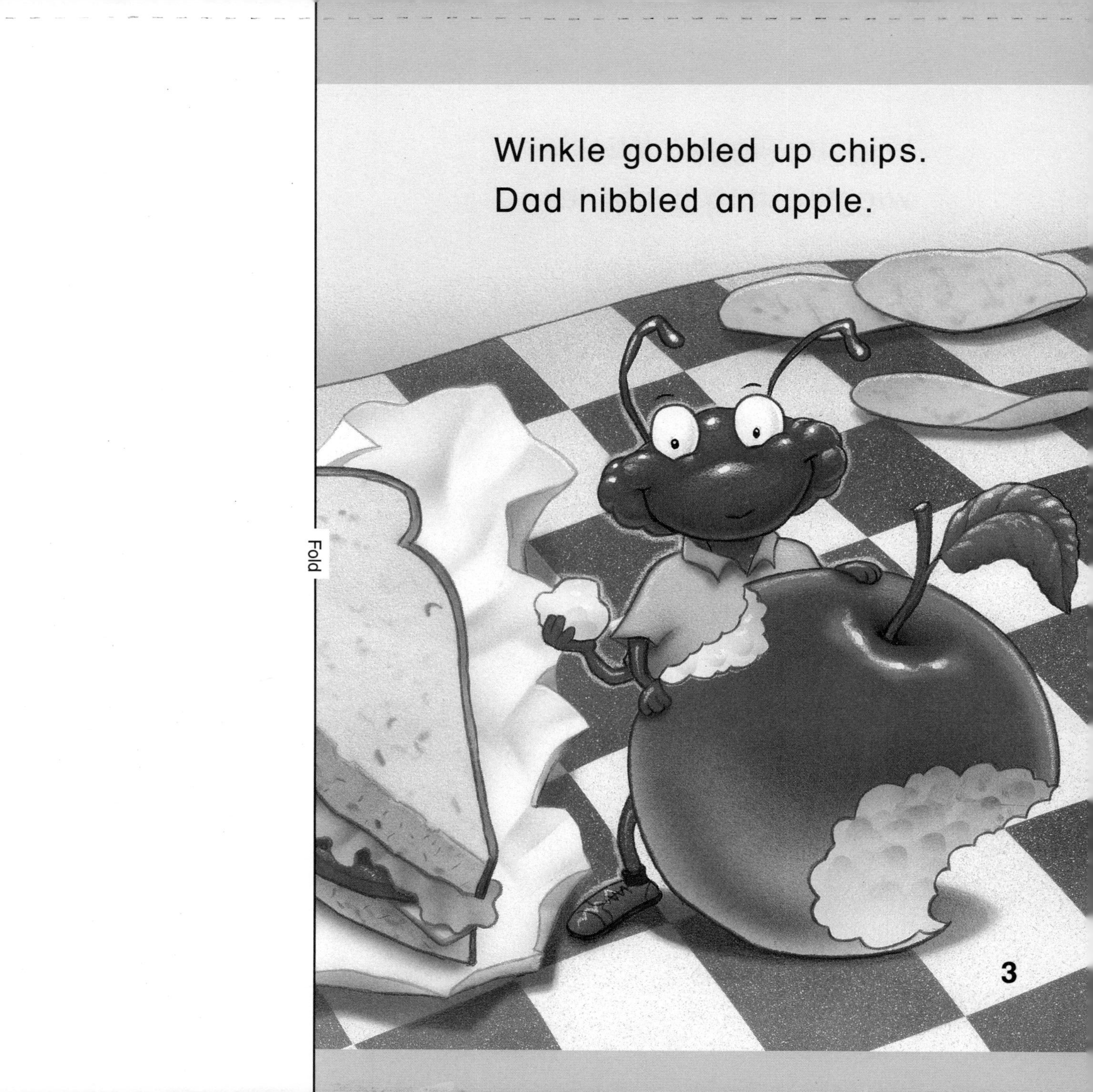

Fold

Wiggle, jiggle. Winkle wiggled into a bottle.

Fold

A Picnic for Winkle

Word Count: 80

High-Frequency Words

into
oh
played
the
to
was

Decodable Words*

a	didn't	had	picnic
an	drip	his	**sparkle**
and	drips	**jiggle**	**sprinkle**
apple	drop	**jingle**	stopped
at	drops	last	swim
bottle	**fiddle**	lit	**twinkle**
but	for	mess	up
candle	**giggle**	**nibble**	went
chips	**gobble**	**nibbled**	**wiggle**
chuckle	**gobbled**	on	**wiggled**
Dad	**grumble**	**paddle**	**Winkle**

*Words with /əl/-*le* appear in **boldface** type.

Giggle, chuckle,
chuckle, giggle!
Dad and Winkle
had a swim!

Fold

Sparkle! Twinkle! Dad lit
the candle and played
a jingle on his fiddle.

Oh! Oh! Drip, drop, sprinkle!
Dad and Winkle had to paddle!

Fold

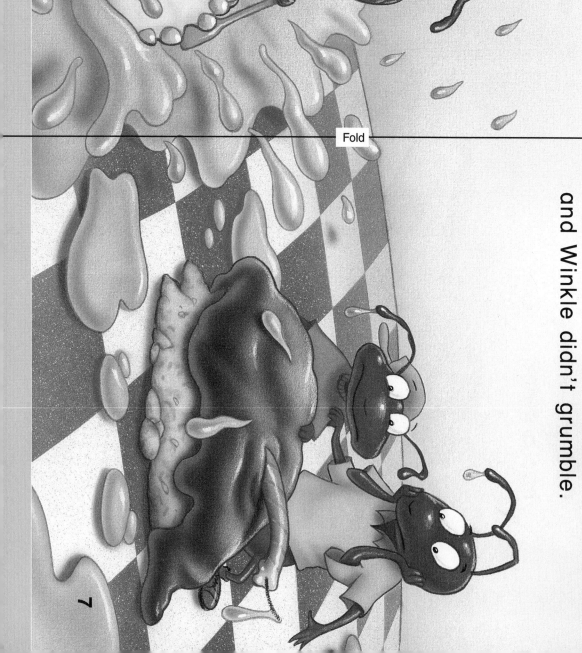

At last the drips and drops stopped.
The picnic was a mess, but Dad
and Winkle didn't grumble.

DECODABLE BOOK 17
Tell Me a Riddle

Fold

Tell Me a Riddle

by Timothy Thomas
illustrated by Monica Gesue

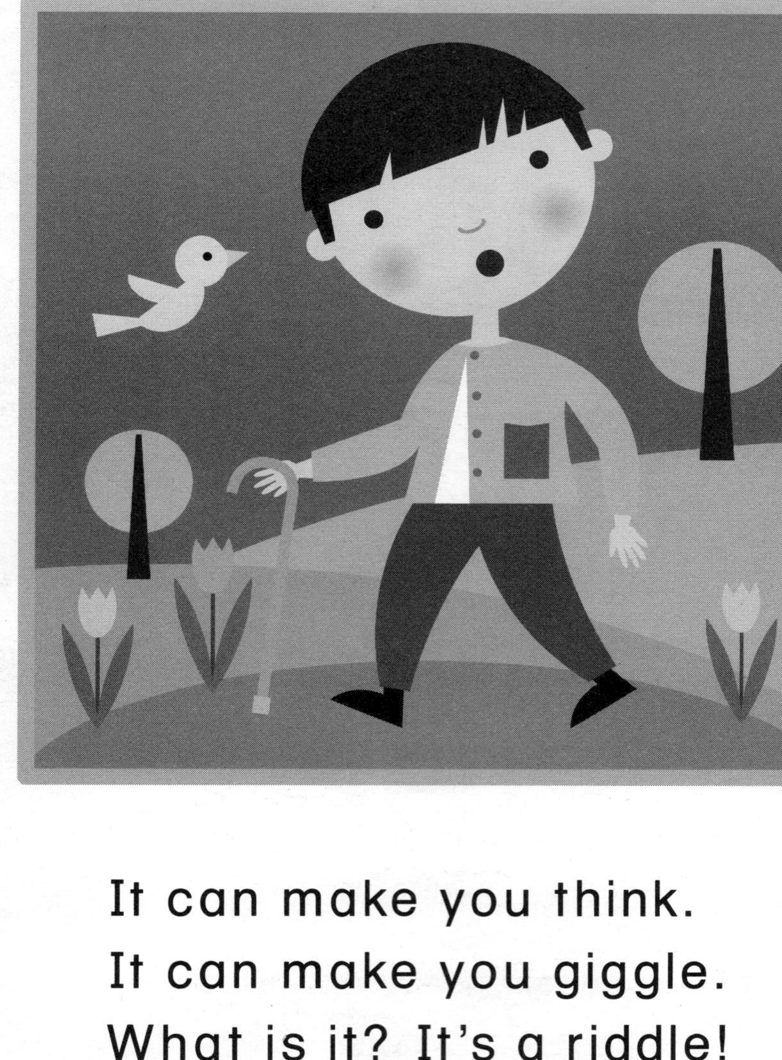

It can make you think.
It can make you giggle.
What is it? It’s a riddle!

Fold

Fold

You can pick it. You can munch it and nibble it. It can startle you if you find a bug in the middle of it! What is it?

It's an apple.

Fold

Tell Me a Riddle

Word Count: 102

High-Frequency Words

find
make
me
of
see
the
what
you
your

Decodable Words*

a	**giggle**	**nibble**	tell
an	if	or	things
and	in	pal	think
apple	is	pet	**tickle**
best	it	pick	toss
bug	it's	**rattle**	**tumble**
but	**jiggle**	**riddle**	up
can	**jumble**	**rumble**	wind
can't	**middle**	**snuggle**	with
cuddle	munch	**startle**	

*Words with /əl/-*le* appear in **boldface** type.

It's a pet.

Fold

You can't see it, but it can rumble. It can make things jiggle and rattle. It can toss and tumble things in a jumble. What is it?

It's the wind.

Fold

You can cuddle it, tickle it, or snuggle up with it. It's your best pal. What is it?

DECODABLE BOOK 18
A Little Fellow

Fold

A Little Fellow

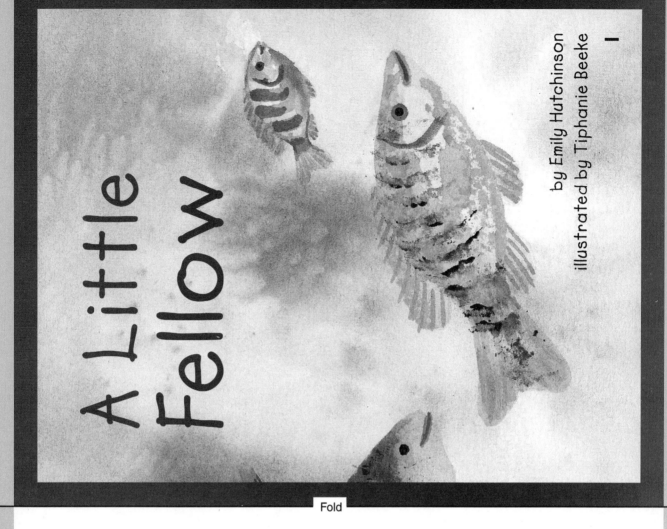

by Emily Hutchinson
illustrated by Tiphanie Beeke

Ellen looks out the window.
“It’s not snowing,” she tells Mom,
“and the wind isn’t blowing.”

Fold

Fold

“Then let’s go fishing,” says Mom. “First bundle up. Put on this thick yellow scarf.”

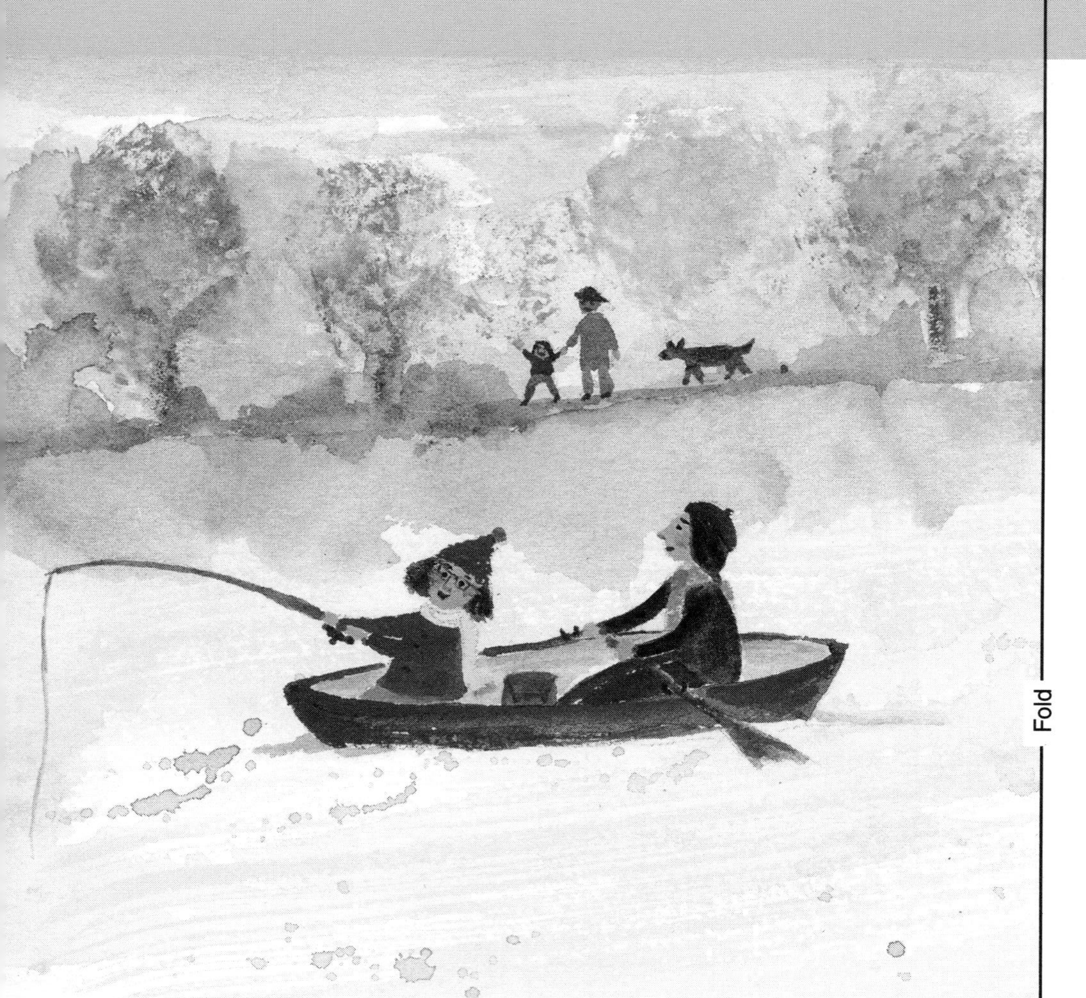

Mom rows and Ellen fishes.

Fold

A Little Fellow

Word Count: 100

High-Frequency Words

day	says
go	sees
good	she
looks	the
out	to
put	

Decodable Words*

a	grins	**slow**
and	**growing**	**snowing**
as	I	soft
back	is	still
blowing	isn't	such
bundle	it	sun
crows	it's	tells
Ellen	just	then
fellow	let's	thick
first	little	this
fish	Mom	**throws**
fishes	not	up
fishing	on	wiggle
flowing	river	wind
for	**rows**	**window**
glowing	scarf	**yellow**
got	**shows**	

*Words with /ō/*ow* appear in **boldface** type.

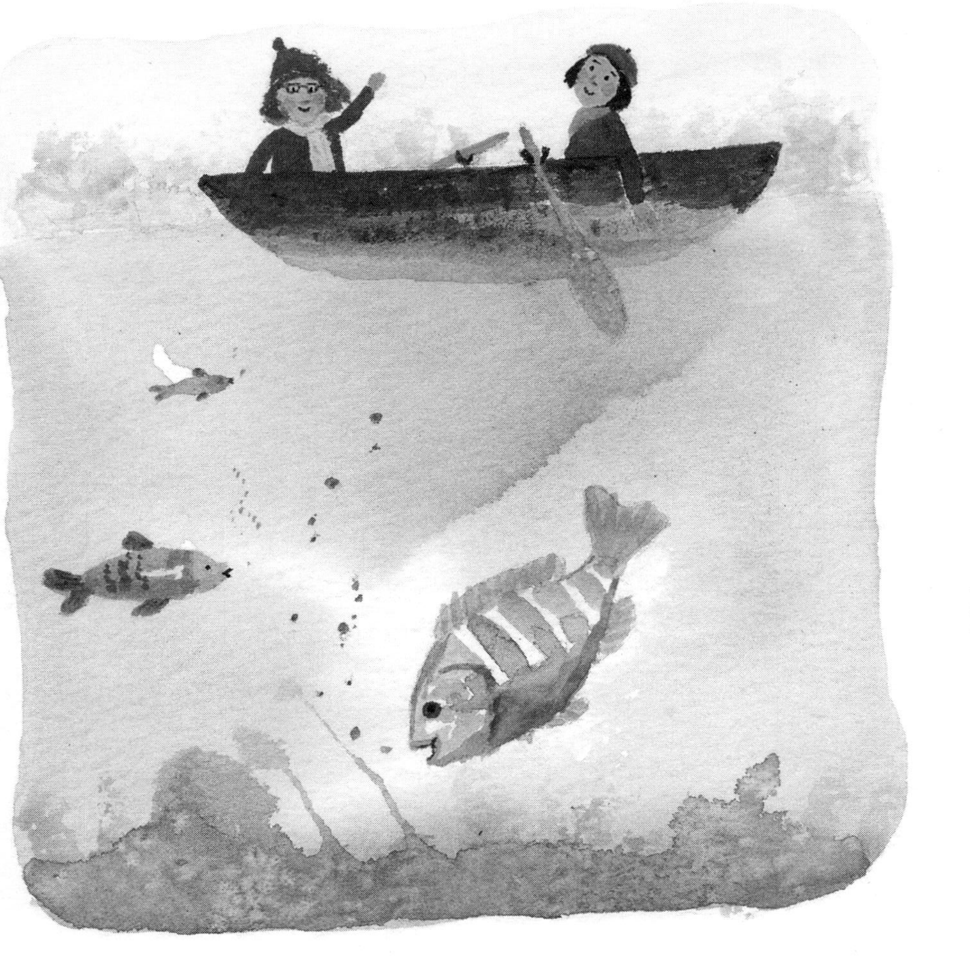

Ellen throws the fish back in the river. Mom just grins.

Fold

"This is a good day for fishing," Mom tells Ellen. "The sun is glowing, and the river is flowing soft and slow."

"I got a fish!" Ellen crows as she shows it to Mom.

Fold

Ellen sees the fish wiggle. "It's such a little fellow!" Ellen tells Mom. "It's still growing!"

DECODABLE BOOK 18
Coal for Gramps

Fold

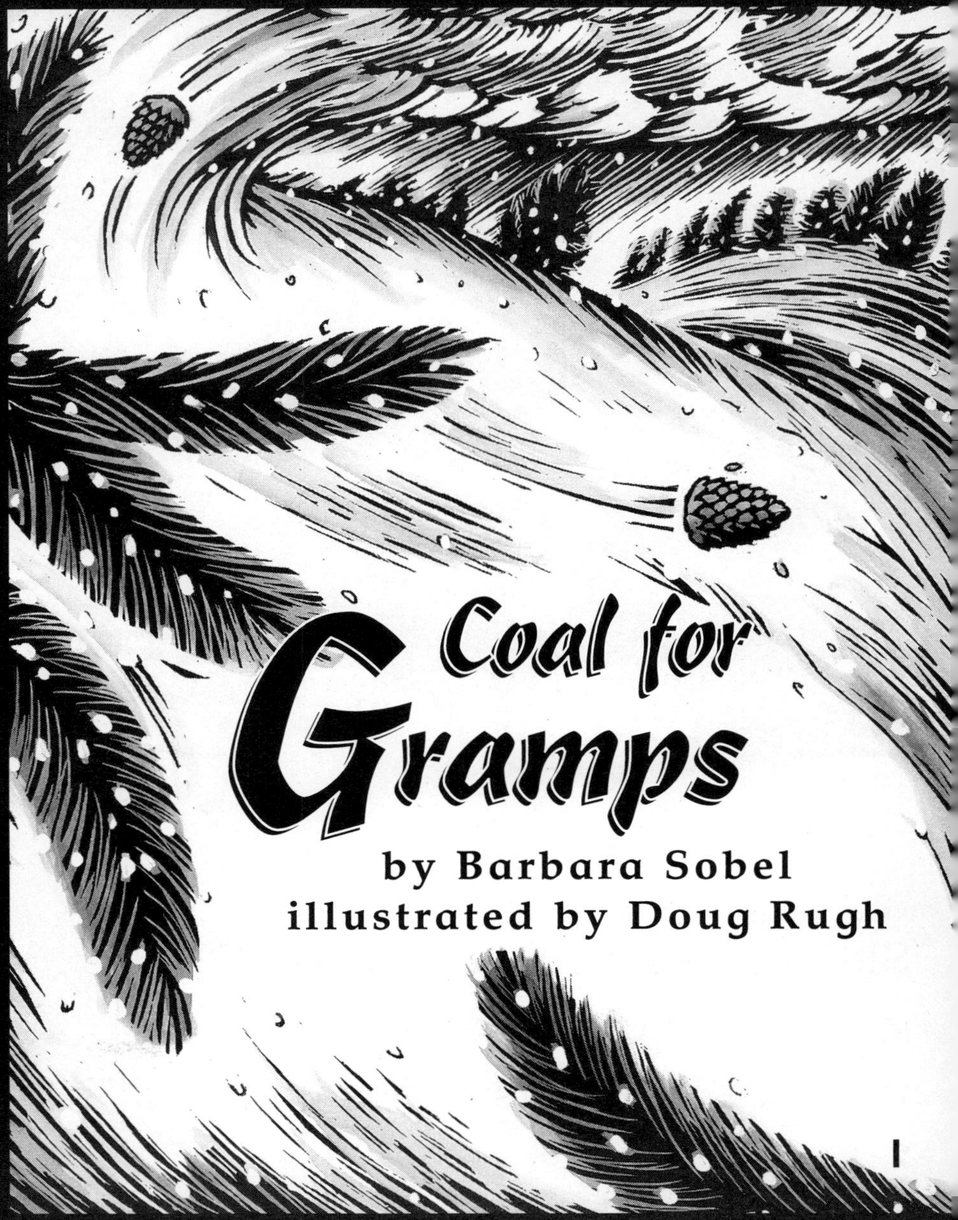

Coal for Gramps

by Barbara Sobel
illustrated by Doug Rugh

Sloan sets a sack on his sled. "This is a load of coal for Gramps," he tells Rex. "Gramps needs this coal!"

Fold

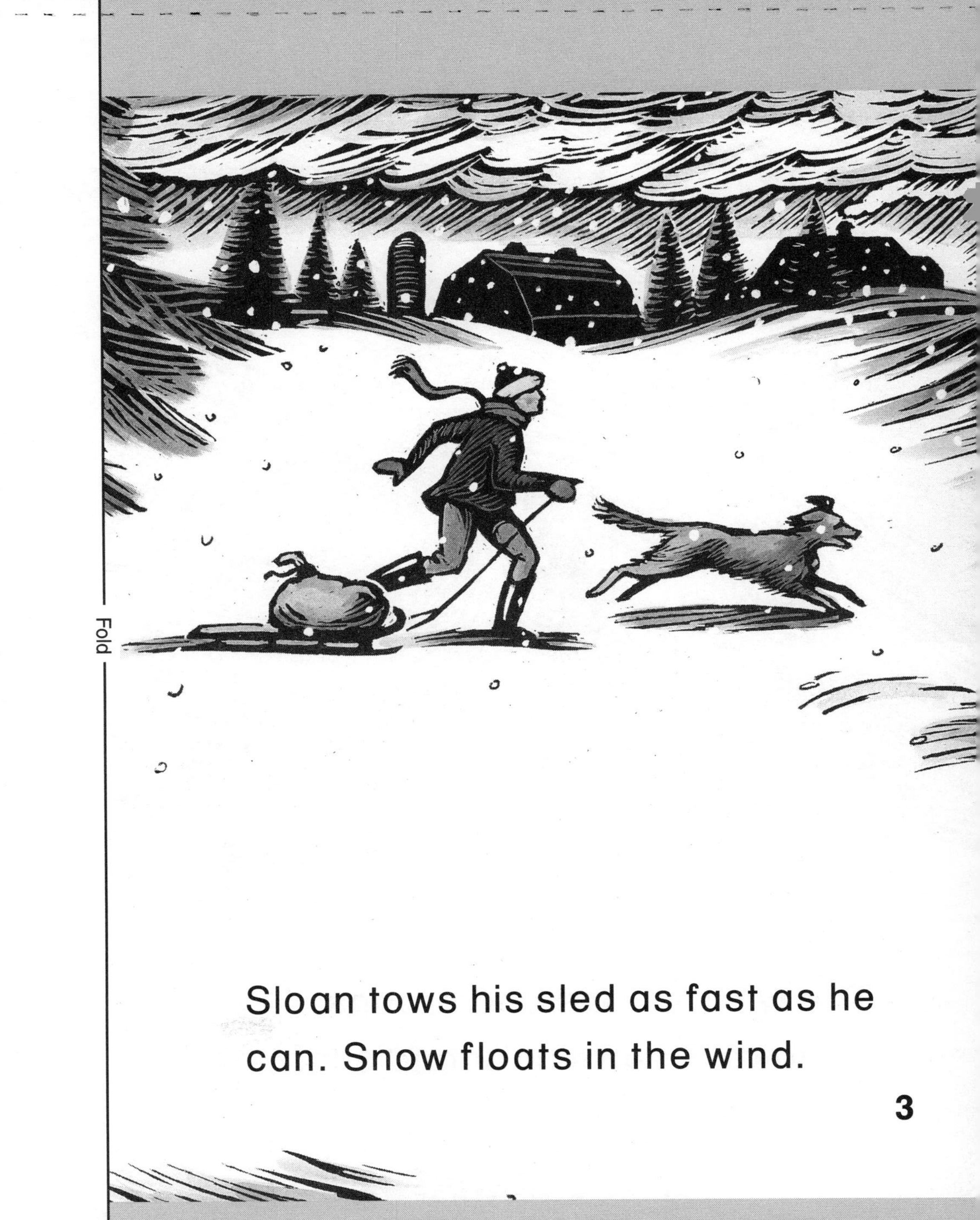

Sloan tows his sled as fast as he can. Snow floats in the wind.

Fold

The wind moans and groans.
It blows Sloan's coat and scarf.

Fold

Coal for Gramps

Word Count: 93

High-Frequency Words

are	see
he	sees
needs	the
of	

Decodable Words*

a	Gramps	scarf
all	**groans**	sets
and	growing	sled
as	harder	**Sloan**
barks	his	**Sloan's**
blows	in	snow
can	is	**soaked**
can't	it	storm
coal	**load**	stronger
coat	lost	sudden
falls	**moans**	tells
fast	on	then
floats	Rex	this
for	**road**	tows
getting	runs	wind
glow	sack	

*Words with /ō/*oa* appear in **boldface** type.

It is Gramps!

The snow falls harder and harder.
Sloan's coat is getting soaked.
The storm is growing stronger.

Sloan can't see the road!
Are Sloan and Rex lost?

All of a sudden, Rex
barks. He sees a glow.
Then Rex runs fast.

DECODABLE BOOK 18
Snowball and Shadow

Fold

Snowball and Shadow

by Emily Hutchinson
illustrated by Margie Moore

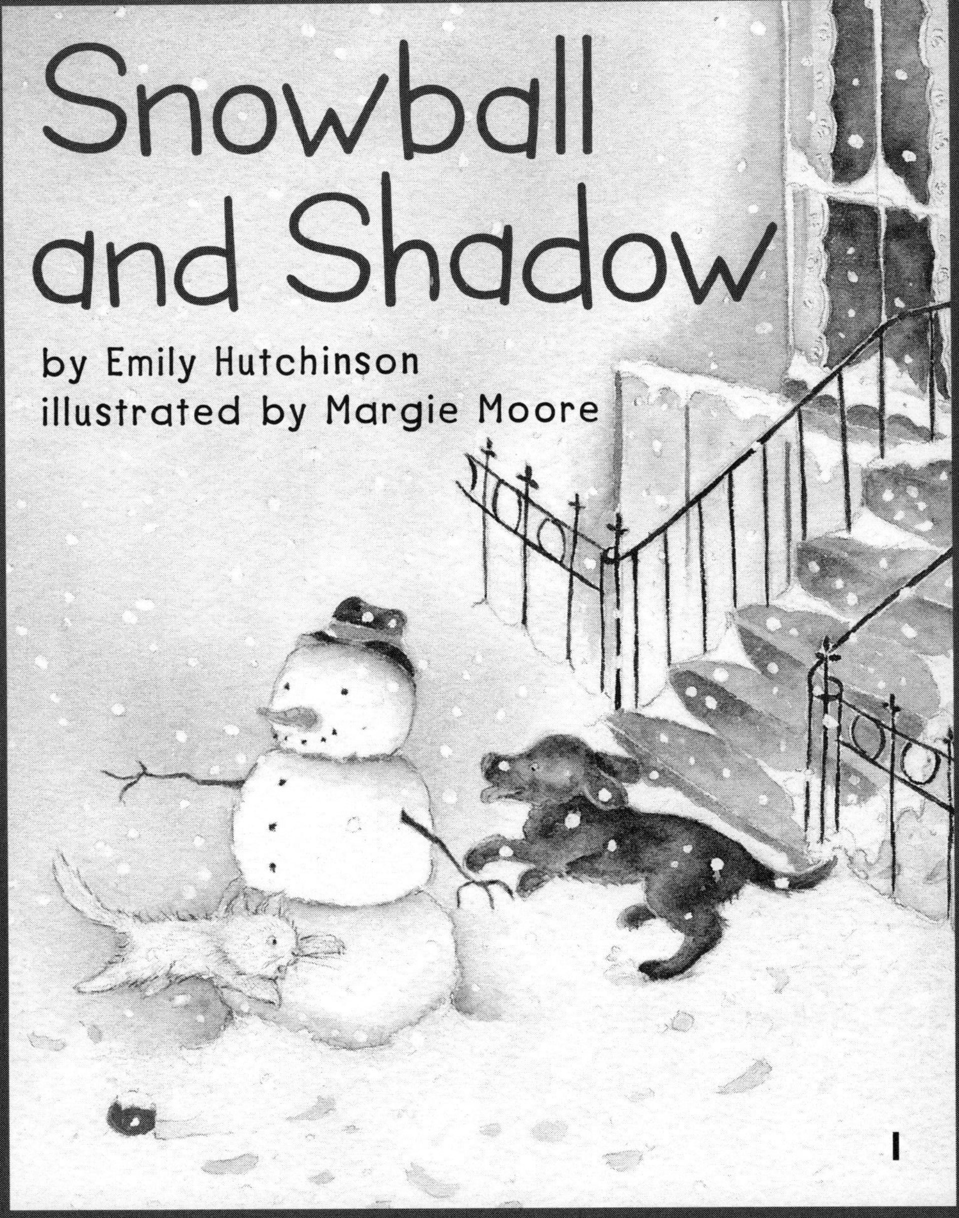

Snowball lives at 15 Crow Road.
Shadow lives at 17 Crow Road.

Fold

Fold

Snowball naps on a soft yellow pillow. Shadow runs and jumps in the snow.

After her nap, Snowball sits up and stretches. She licks her flowing fur until it glows.

Fold

Snowball and Shadow

Word Count: 97

High-Frequency Words

find	of	where
he	out	
knows	she	
lives	the	
looks	to	

Decodable Words*

a	in	sits
after	is	sniffing
and	it	**snow**
at	jumps	**Snowball**
ball	licks	**snowman**
can't	nap	soft
Crow	naps	stretches
dashes	off	that
digging	on	**throws**
fetch	**owner**	top
flowing	**pillow**	trots
follows	purrs	until
fur	Road	up
glows	runs	**window**
her	**Shadow**	**yellow**
hops	**Shadow's**	

*Words with /ō/*ow* appear in **boldface** type.

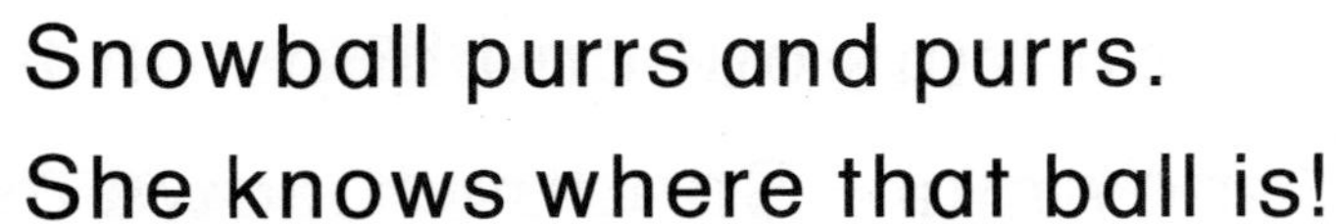

Snowball purrs and purrs.
She knows where that ball is!

Fold

Shadow's owner throws a ball.
Shadow dashes off to fetch it.

Snowball looks out the window. Shadow is sniffing and digging in the snow. He can't find the ball!

Fold

Snowball trots out and hops on top of a snowman. Shadow follows her.

DECODABLE BOOK 18
Camping at Oak Pond

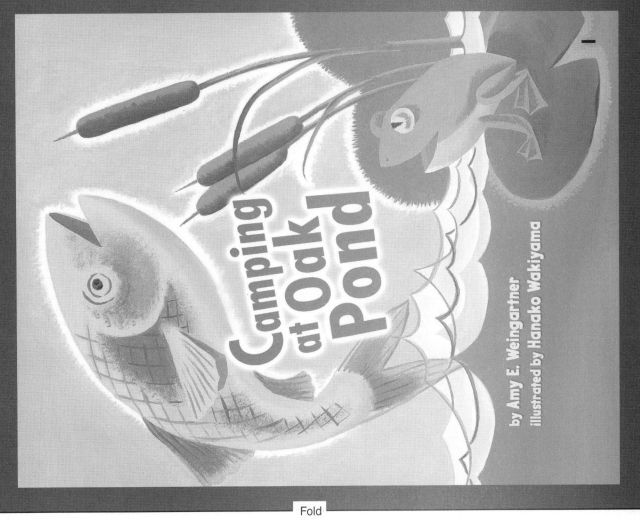

Fold

Camping at Oak Pond

by Amy E. Weingartner
illustrated by Hanako Wakiyama

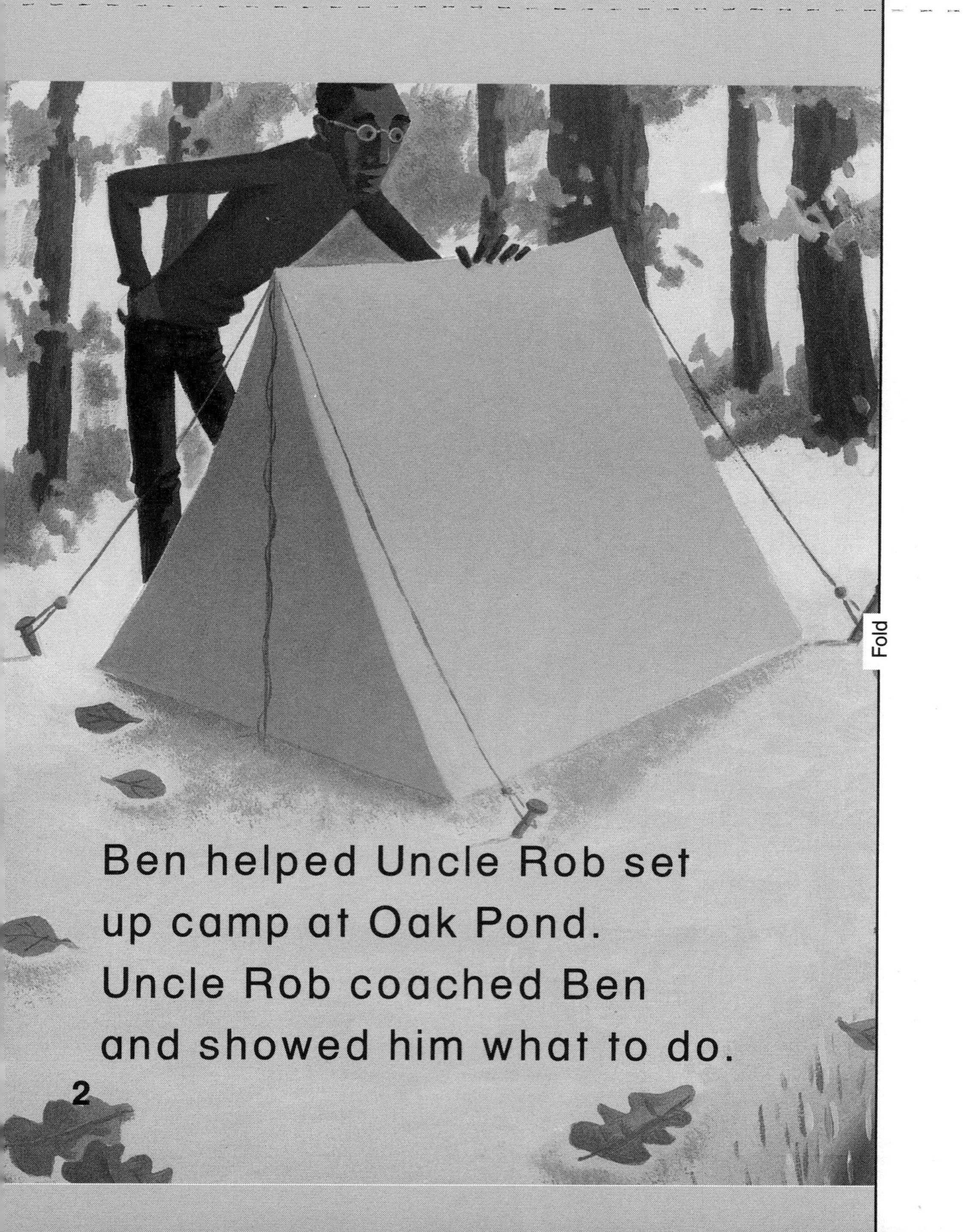

Ben helped Uncle Rob set
up camp at Oak Pond.
Uncle Rob coached Ben
and showed him what to do.

Fold

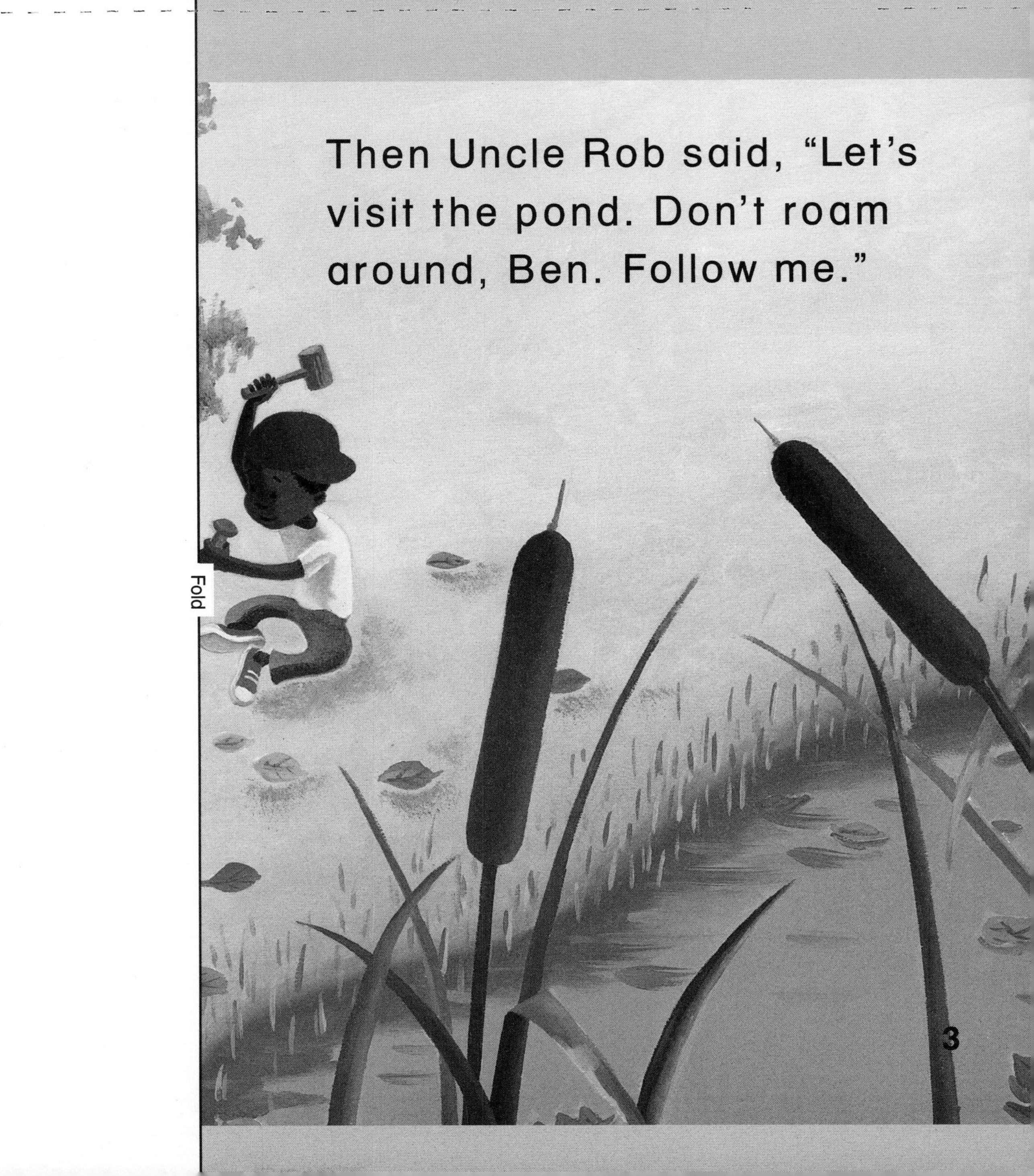

Then Uncle Rob said, “Let’s visit the pond. Don’t roam around, Ben. Follow me.”

Fold

Croak! Croak! Splash! "Look at that toad!" yelled Ben. "Its throat is all puffed up."

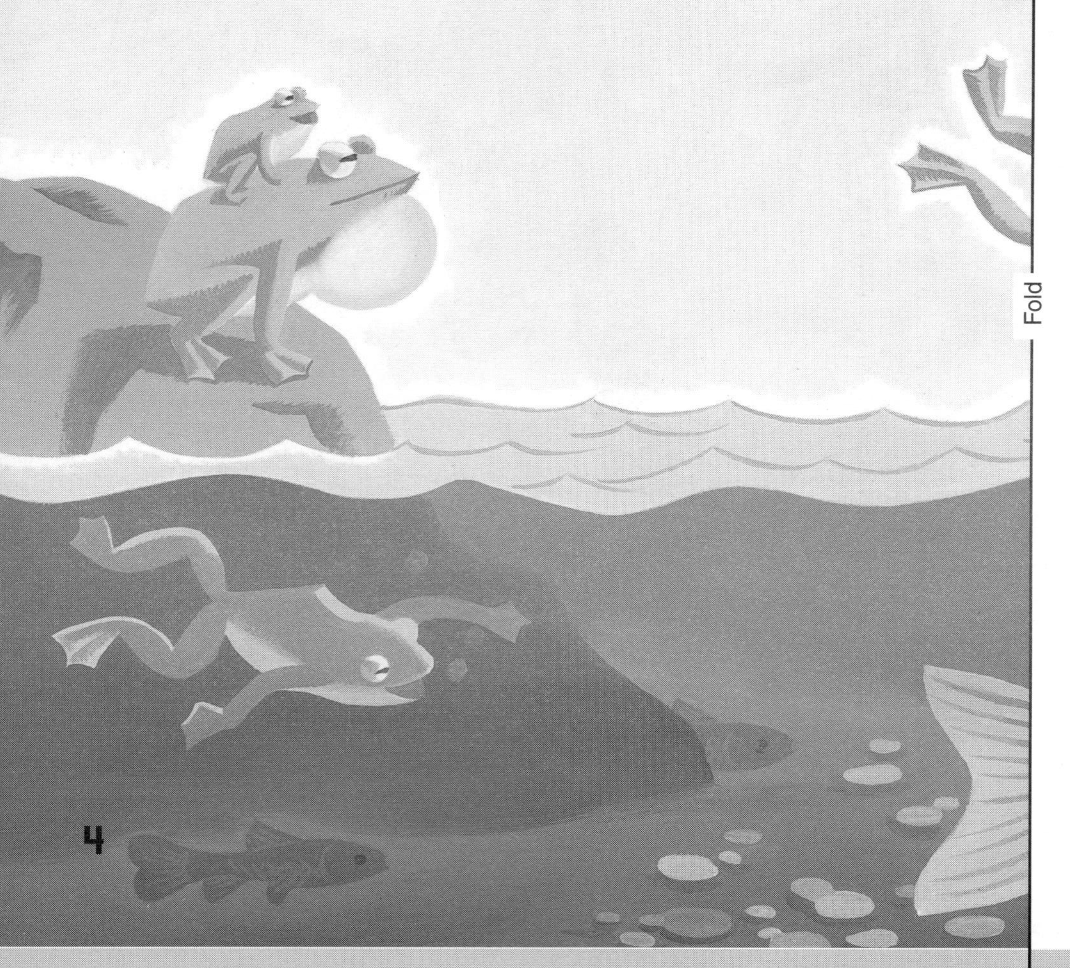

Fold

Camping at Oak Pond

Word Cound: 101

High-Frequency Words

around	now
do	oh
don't	said
like	the
look	to
looks	was
me	what
no	what's

Decodable Words*

a	fish	its	slip
all	**floating**	it's	**soaked**
and	**foam**	let's	splash
asked	follow	not	that
at	frog	**oak**	then
Ben	fun	on	**throat**
camp	giggled	pond	**toad**
camping	**groaned**	puffed	Uncle
coached	helped	**roam**	up
croak	him	Rob	visit
croaking	is	set	yelled
eggs	it	showed	

*Words with /ō/*oa* appear in **boldface** type.

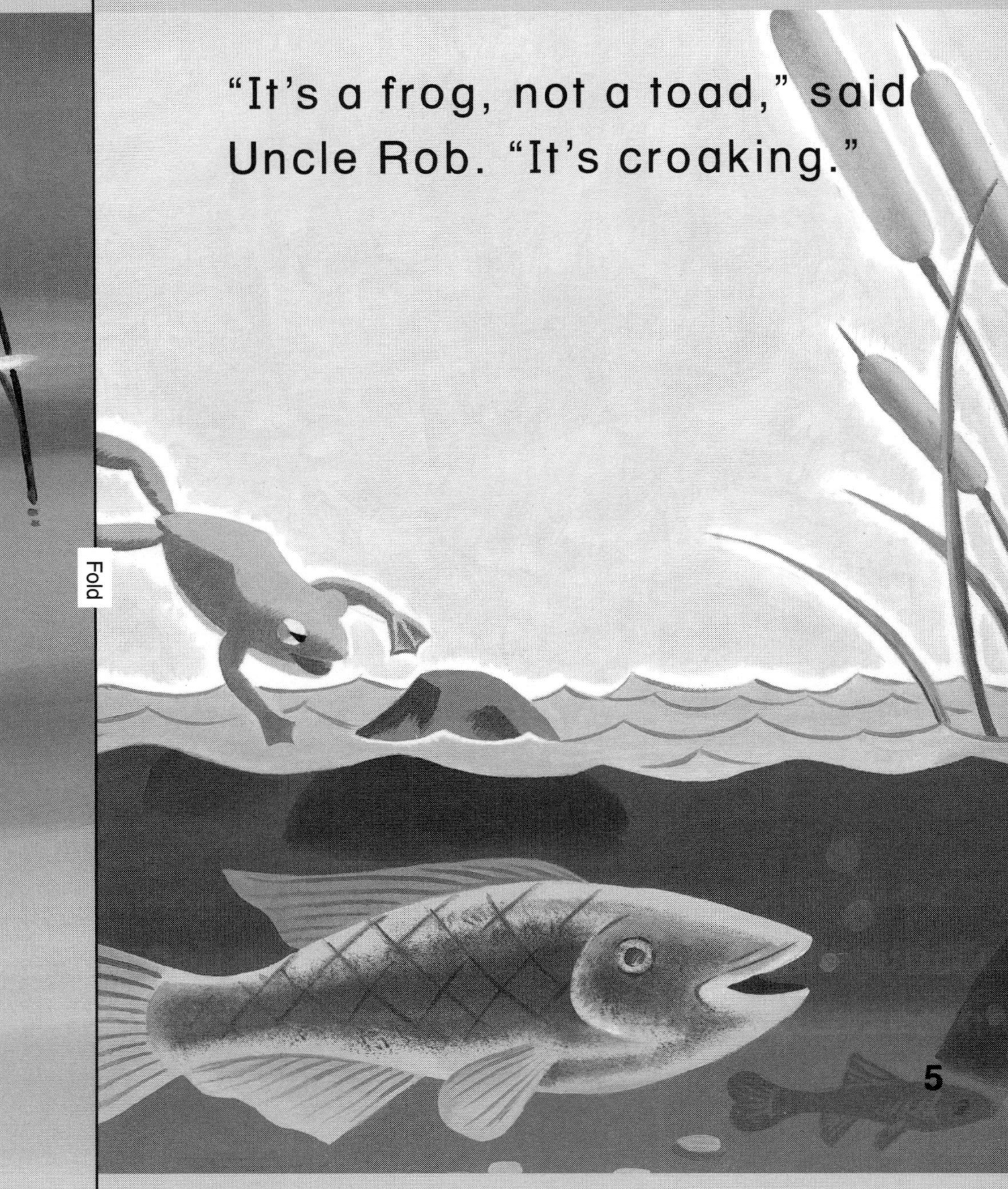

Slip! Splash! Ben was soaked!
"Oh, no!" groaned Uncle Rob.
"Camping is fun!" Ben giggled.

Fold

"It's a frog, not a toad," said Uncle Rob. "It's croaking."

"What's that?" asked Ben. "It looks like foam floating on the pond."

"It's fish eggs," said Uncle Rob. "Now don't slip, Ben!"